PLAYING RIGHT FIELD

GEORGE TABB

Playing Right Field
A Jew Grows in Greenwich

By George Tabb

Soft Skull Press | 2004

© 2004 by George Tabb

Published by Soft Skull Press
71 Bond Street, Brooklyn, NY 11217

Distributed by Publishers Group West
1.800.788.3123 | www.pgw.com

Printed in Canada

Library of Congress Cataloging-in-Publication Data for this title
available from the Library of Congress.

For Wendy, Nick, my brothers,
and, of course, My Mom

CONTENTS

INTRODUCTION

GEORGE TABB IS A PUSSY.

A huge pussy. Maybe the biggest pussy in the annals of punk rock, which is saying a lot.

Everybody knows he's a pussy. His lovely wife Wendy knows it. His Yorkie P.J. ("Pussy Junior"), who happens to be my god-dog, knows it. The armies of punk rock kids who've been fans of Furious George over the years, and look up to him like a wayward and way-cool big brother, know it. All of his friends know it. All of his enemies, too.

Yes, George is a total pussy. And everybody, except probably for his enemies, loves him for it.

Because George is a sweetheart. One of the nicest, sweetest guys in the world. For all that he loves playing bloody video games and banging out the punk rock, in real life he wouldn't hurt a flea. A total softy.

He's also one of the funniest people I know. Which is usually how he makes enemies. Some people just have no sense of humor. They get hurt or angry when he jokes around about, say, women in rock. They're so pretentious and politically correct and closed-minded that they can't tell he's only fooling around and trying to get a rise out of them. They take the bait every time. Some people who like to think they're really smart can be really, really stupid that way.

The first reminiscence of George's I read that had me literally falling out of my chair laughing was about auditioning to be the new bassist in his beloved Ramones. George was, and probably always will be, the world's most devoted fan of the Ramones, and even though he didn't get the gig the guys in the band always acted like he was kind of the Fifth Ramone. Like all of George's writing, the piece was not only hilarious but touching and heartbreaking and disarmingly stoopit and tinged with a sweet sadness.

But it didn't answer the crucial question: Why is George Tabb such a pussy?

For that, you have to read his tales of childhood and growing up, like the ones in this book. George has crystal clear memories of his childhood, and as well as anyone currently writing he knows how to evoke, in simple and kidlike language, the humor and the horror and the mysteries and joys and brutalities and confusion and powerlessness and plain dorkness of being a kid.

No doubt George's memories are so sharp because his growing-up years were so rocky. You'll see it in these pages, some of it sadly universal, some of it stories only George Tabb could tell. He endured a lot. His parents' divorce, and having to live with the shrewish stepmom and the perpetually angry dad. The too-short visits with his real mom and loving stepfather Nick. Defying death at Coney Island and at summer camp. The constant need to stand up to antisemitic bullies (even the blind kid and the one-armed kid kicked his ass). Faking it in the school band. Puking, crying, shitting his pants in public. Embarrassing ballgames. Embarrassing boners. Plus: exploding frogs, flaming mice, split kittens, bloody deer carcasses, a monstrous turtle and a huge, humping canine.

There's more, and no doubt George'll get to it all in future volumes.

What a childhood. It's no wonder he's such a puss. The wonder is how he also turned out to be such a great guy. And that he can wring so many very funny scenes out of all that torment and torture.

I think that's why all those punk-rock kids love him so. George knows how fucked up being a kid can be. But he can laugh about it, and get them to laugh with him. He's the underdog's underdog, triumphant. The best song Furious George ever played, the band's de facto anthem, has four simple lines of verse:

> I wear a white hat
> I wear a red shirt
> They all think I'm stupid
> One day I'll kill them

And then came the chorus, an angry and menacing cheer, and the kids in the audience would get up on stage and chant it along with George:

> I'M GILLIGAN. I'M GILLIGAN.
> I'M GILLIGAN. I'M GILLIGAN.

It was silly and goony, and it looked awfully liberating and fun.

*

On September 11, 2001, George and Wendy Tabb stood at the windows of their apartment and watched the World Trade Center towers burn a few blocks away. They saw people leap from the windows, and heard the horrifying sound their bodies made exploding on impact far below. They grabbed P.J. and ran from the evil, boiling cloud of smoke and dust that roared up the streets of lower

Manhattan when the buildings collapsed.

George, Wendy and P.J. crashed that night at Nick's apartment in the West Village. When they visited their place a few days later, they found that the ventilation system had sucked a fine powder of dust and ash into the building. Every surface in their apartment was coated with the ashes of the pulverized WTC towers. Something in the air made them feel physically ill, so they returned to Nick's—where they remained for over a year.

During that year, George and Wendy were all over the national and international media declaring their strong suspicions that the dust and debris from the fallen towers represented real health hazards that the government wasn't taking seriously. More and more workers at the WTC site, and residents as far away as Brooklyn (where the winds had carried the debris cloud), reported symptoms similar to those the Tabbs had experienced. Meanwhile, the EPA kept insisting that there were no health risks. The New York City media were peculiarly dismissive, one columnist sneering that the Tabbs shouldn't be heard because they weren't experts in medicine or the environmental sciences. (Neither were miners' canaries, but the miners didn't quibble.) People who owned homes or businesses near the site, justifiably worried about property values if word got out that the neighborhood could make you sick, told the Tabbs and the others to shut up. They said the complainers were just being hysterical. That George was, in effect, a pussy.

It all must have felt quite familiar to him.

But, as he often does in the stories in this book, George eventually triumphed over the bullies. Sort of. It's become increasingly evident that the government stonewalled and covered up potential health risks after 9/11, as it did many other aspects of the event. Over time, as the government is forced to release more of the data

it suppressed, and proper epidemiological studies can be conduct-
ed, I personally am confident that the Tabbs will be vindicated.

Not that it will do them much good. In 2003, well over a year
after they'd abandoned their apartment, the government finally
sent a team to examine it. They took one look around, bagged all
the Tabbs' furniture and belongings, and carted it all away to a
toxic waste dump.

By that point, George and Wendy were done with New York
City. They moved to Phoenix, Arizona, where Wendy and P.J. are
enjoying the hot, sunny weather, and George enjoys eyeing all the
tanned blondes with their bouncy boob-jobs. They have a house
and a car, and George still gets to play lots of video games. The
friends they left back here in NYC miss them a lot, but I don't
think any of us begrudge them a little piece of mind.

As long as George doesn't make good on his threat to re-form
Furious George and take it on the road again.

Pussy.

> *John Strausbaugh*
> *NYC*
> *December 2003*

John Strausbaugh is the author of Rock 'Til You Drop. *He lives in
Brooklyn.*

RIDE THE BUS

SO THERE I WAS, IN the second grade, and every morning at the corner of Londonderry Drive and Stanwich Road, our bus stop, when it started.

He would be there, ready. Waiting for me. And later, for my brothers.

His name was Mark.

Mark Healy.

My introduction to the next decade of my life.

I'll never forget the first three words he spoke to me from behind his wavy blondish hair and steel blue-green eyes.

"You're a Jew!"

And then came the fists.

*

The Tabb boys learned early on how to fight.

Or flee.

Having been born before Luke and Sam, the way I saw it was I had no choice. If the bullies didn't pick on me, they'd go after them. So I learned to fight.

Well, get beat-up.

Being small for my age, kicking my ass wasn't much of an

accomplishment. But the shit-heels in Greenwich thought it was. And, apparently, so did their parents.

Especially Mark Healy's.

"You're nothing but a dirty Jew," Mark would say to me most weekday mornings. Thankfully, I had the weekends off.

"Dirty?" I would ask him, totally confused.

I could understand the "Jew" part. A little. My grandfather once explained to me why we had to wear those funny little hats at some family get-togethers. But the "dirty" part threw me for a loop. I took lots of showers. And still do. Filth and I don't get along.

"Yeah," Mark would sneer, "you're nothing but a low-down, curly-haired, hook-nosed, dirty Jew-boy!"

And every time I'd try to ask him what he meant, it was always too late. He'd grab my Batman lunch box, with the Bat-cycle on the outside of the thermos, and smash it open on the concrete of Londonderry Drive.

"You're mommy packs lunch for you," he'd say, "and I unpack it!"

He would then take out my bologna sandwich (with mustard on one side), apple, and three Oreo Cookies and toss them as hard as he could into the woods.

"What ya gonna do about it, Tabb?" he would ask.

I kept quiet. What could I say? He was in sixth grade and I was in second. Plus he was at least a couple of feet taller than me.

"You gonna cry you little pussy?" Healy would continue.

Of course I tried not to, but my tears would always betray me.

Finally, I'd usually tell him to "Stop it!" and then the poundings would begin. He'd tighten his fist and punch me as hard as he could in the nose. The largest and easiest target. After I'd start to bleed, he'd laugh, then kick me in the stomach, followed by a right hook to the chin. That's when I'd usually bite my tongue or lip, and bleed some more. By the time the school bus would arrive, I'd be lunch-less and swollen-faced.

Loosened up for round two. My stepsister, Diane, would just stand there in shock. Then he'd pour out my Kool-aid, and toss the empty thermos and lunch box. I would just look at him with my wet blue eyes.

*

And so it began.

The violence, the beatings, the bashed bologna sandwiches and, of course, the bus fights.

After my first four-year stint in Brooklyn, New York, as a bed-wetter and overweight blanket-baby, my parents moved us to Muttentown, Long Island, where they quickly divorced (my mom leaving my dad). What followed was a fast move to Greenwich, Connecticut, where my dad "obtained" custody of us kids by bribing a judge. That's how his world worked in the late-sixties era of insider trading and bullying big business.

Things were a bit different in Greenwich.

But not totally.

There was big business, and bullies—but the one thing the richest suburb in the United States lacked was Jews. Sure there may have been a handful of them, but they hid themselves well amongst the pasty faces of the blonde-haired blue-eyed masses. Greenwich didn't like Jews, but for some reason, my father liked Greenwich.

The one thing that became clear over time, is that if he was thinking of us it was only to move us as far away from my mom as possible. Myself and Luke and Sam. Us boys, and my two stepsisters, Diane and Tina, and future half-sister, Stephanie, seemed to be along for the ride. Of course with my father, Lester, at the helm, and Cybil, my stepmother as first-mate, the positions we filled were just lowly pirates. But we'll get to that. Later.

For now, we'll start with the bus. Or better yet, the bus stop where we'd hike a mile to each morning. My father had told us we had it easy, that he "hiked" five miles to school every morning.

In Brooklyn, New York.

Years later I found out it was five minutes.

Whatever. Maybe he wanted to give us a better education.

Maybe he thought he'd network well with the corporate kings of America. Or maybe he just wanted to show off his obscene amount of cash by buying fourteen acres of prime real estate to house his antique car collection, seven horses, and new trophy wife who already had two daughters.

*

When Luke, Sam, and I would get on the bus, it was time for the Tabb family beating. There were these two little fuckers in particular, Joe and Katy Klaus, who really would give it to us good. I remember the sister, Katy, hitting me with a fist, with her index finger slightly raised, and yelling "get the point, Tabb, get the point?"

Meanwhile, Joe would be hitting Luke and Sam while they cried for help. The bus driver, Jackie, ignored what was going on, and kept smoking pot as she drove us to Parkway Elementary school. She'd be listening to songs like "Joy to the World," and every time the kids would get louder than her radio, she'd throw back a handful of candy, which would amuse the little shits for a while, at least until the song was over. Then she'd throw some more. She also raced the bus like a speed-demon, which all the kids loved, of course.

So, we'd be there getting beat up, and our hippie bus driver wouldn't help. You'd think other kids would jump in, or at least yell for the beatings to stop, but most of the kids on our bus just shouted, "kill the Jews, kill the Jews."

Thanks Dad, for moving us to such a nice town.

Later my father tried to have our family join the Burning Tree Country Club, the same place these kids hung out after school and on weekends. Thankfully, we weren't allowed in because of our religious and racial status. Jewish. But that's okay, they didn't allow any blacks in either. Of course, there weren't any around, except for the housekeepers and maids. Burning Cross Country Club would have made a much better name.

While the Klaus's would start them, a lot of other kids on the bus would join in on the beatings, if they felt so inclined. Kids like Marc Newsted, his older brother J.P., Ricky Emmerson, and Bruno Pierre, the D'Angelo brothers, and lots more. We'd get to school all bloody and stuff, but were warned that if we ever told a teacher, we would be killed. So we used to say that we fell down some stairs, or banged into something by accident, like we did when our father would go to town on us.

Anyway, I forget when it was, maybe fifth or sixth grade, but I, for one, had had enough. Luke, Sam, and I decided that it was time to take some action. Our father had tried to teach us how to box, but that doesn't work against a bunch of kids fixated on their parents' belief that we belonged in the gas chamber. Plus, as it turns out, my dad didn't know how to box, just how to wear women's underwear. So we found ourselves having to do something, and the D'Angelo brothers were our fist target.

Tony and Paulie. Paulie was the younger and smaller of the two. Their father must have been some mob guy who made it big and got his family a house in Greenwich. They had a big, white

Cadillac, which their mother drove at awesome speeds up and down Londonderry Drive. All the kids called her "Speed Queen." Tony and Paulie called her "Mama."

These kids were real pieces of work. They had new shoes every day, and each owned like fifty suits or something. They were dressed up like good little goodfellas, and even had the accents to go with it. Tony would say to me, "Hey Tabb, if you don't let Paulie beat up Sam, I'm gonna give you a pair of cement shoes."

I'd say, "I'd rather have the ones you're wearing," which usually resulted in a split lip. This would go on day after day after day. I remember once their father came on our school bus and told us Tabb boys to "Stop fucking with my sons' suits, capiche?" We later told this to our father and stepmother who quickly replied, "Fight your own battles."

Fuck 'em.

So, one day, in the middle of the winter, Luke, Sam and I reached the end of our ropes. The D'Angelos started in on their mini-mobster routine, and my brothers and I took action. Tony started hitting Luke, and Paulie, Sam. All the kids were yelling, and Jackie just kept throwing back more and more candy. I got Tony's attention by calling him a "Dayglo," and he came after me, saying, "You're dead, Tabb, you're really dead." Tony's little brother, who I guess got bored with beating up Sam, joined in. As they started to hit me, I motioned for Sam and Luke to do their thing. They went to the back of the bus and opened the emergency door. It was snowing hard outside, so the bus wasn't going over fifty that day. I then bum-rushed the two wise guys and pushed them out of the back of the bus. While it was moving.

They landed in the middle of the street, and all the kids started laughing and clapping.

Violence was violence.

We closed the door, and then promptly took our seats. Jackie threw back some more candy, not even knowing that she had just dropped off two of Parkway's students on their way to class.

When we arrived at school we were asked to go to the principal's office, not to pass go, and not to collect two hundred dollars.

Obviously someone had told. We waited in the stale wood-paneled room until the D'Angelos arrived with their parents, then for Cybil and Lester, who took their sweet time.

When everyone was present, the D'Angelos started the ball rolling by saying that the "Tabbs were rotten apples." The principal, recovering from a recent mental breakdown, then asked who the "instigators" were. The D'Angelos' reply?

"The Jews."

Of course I then told everyone our side of the story. How we were beaten day in and day out, and how we had finally had enough. It was decided that, to make things fair, all the kids involved would not be allowed to ride the bus for three weeks.

My stepmother, pissed as hell that now she couldn't stay home in the mornings listening to Carole King or fucking the carpenter, yelled at us for the next few weeks. My dad got so angry about my stepmother yelling, he grounded us for a month.

And beat the shit out of me.

But we were victorious. The bus-beatings to Parkway slowly faded away after the D'Angelo debacle. We showed 'em that the Tabbs had had enough. Even the Klaus's almost left us alone. In fact, years later, I saw Joe Klaus hitchhiking, and picked him up in my dad's station wagon. He was on his way to work, at a local gas station. He had dropped out of school in the tenth grade, and was trying to help support his and his girlfriend's baby. He told me I somehow looked familiar, but didn't know where he knew me from. I told him he looked familiar too, but that we had probably never met. I dropped him off at work and he said I seemed like a nice guy, and it was nice meeting me. That was the last I ever saw of him.

*

The next major bus fight I got into was two years later in the seventh grade, when Bruno Pierre and Ricky Emmerson started to beat me up on a regular basis. I was in junior high, and my brothers, who were younger, weren't around yet. It was just me now.

Bruno was this overly big French guy with a Pepe LePew accent, and Ricky was this weasely white-haired kid who looked like a cross between Marty Feldman and Speedy Gonzalez.

Real creepy.

They'd gotten into a routine of beating me up on the bus every day after school. They'd throw my books out the school-bus window and slap me around like their little prison bitch. Of course they couldn't do it without all the Jew insults, which, by this time, had grown a bit tiresome.

Finally, one day, I snapped. I got on the bus ready to fight. I'd done a bunch of push-ups in gym right before the last bell and was pumped up for the showdown.

They started in with the big nose/ little boy stuff, calling me a faggot for carrying a lunch box. So I hit Ricky Emmerson with it so hard his left eye started bleeding, later needing eight stitches. I also hit Bruno in his big fat French nose and laughed while he stood there in shock, blood pouring from his nostrils into his mouth.

Of course, after that incident, we no longer fought. In fact, we started to hang out together. Bruno would take me fishing and soon became a valuable bodyguard, while Ricky gave me my first porno magazine.

Later, I think we went camping.

After I left Greenwich, I grew to miss those guys.

Some of the others, too.

A JEW VS. JESUS

RELIGIOUS SYMBOLS AND THE CONCEPT of evil fascinated me when I was a little kid. I remember seeing *Rosemary's Baby* and *The Omen*, and feeling something that wasn't fear.

It was jealousy.

I wanted to be Mia Farrow's devilish offspring. I wanted to be Damien, to have cool dogs around me, to kill people with plates of glass. I especially wanted to be Damien in *Omen II*, where he went to boarding school and killed tons of bullies.

No such luck. I was stuck being a Jew in Greenwich, Connecticut. The only antichrists around were the other kids, who kicked my ass every day.

But in the fifth grade things changed. I met a kid named Jimmy Foster and he didn't kick my ass. In fact, he sort of, well, liked me. He liked me enough to invite me to sleep over at his house one night.

A night I will never forget. A night I learned about true evil.

*

"Mom," says Jimmy, as we both enter his huge house on Roundhouse Road one Friday afternoon after school," this is my friend George. He's the one who's gonna sleep over."

"Hello George," says Mrs. Foster, "It's nice to see Jimmy has a friend. Please make yourself at home."

"Has a friend?" I say to Jimmy.

"My mom is weird," whispers Jimmy.

"Oh," I reply.

"Jimmy," says Mrs. Foster, "why don't you and little George here go and change into some play clothes. Your father will be home for dinner around seven, and then we'll all eat. You do like venison, don't you George?"

"Um," I stammer. I was afraid to tell her I hated fish.

"It's deer meat," exclaims Jimmy, seeing that I was confused, "and guess what?"

"What?" I say in a high-pitched squeak.

"My dad killed it himself!" says Jimmy.

"Oh," I say, shocked.

We make our way through the kitchen, to Jimmy's room. On the way, I see plenty of Jesus pictures hanging all over the place, as well as over a dozen deer heads in the living room.

"My dad killed all those bucks," explains Jimmy.

I look at all the stationary heads staring blankly at me, with their pitch-black eyes.

"Really?" I ask.

"Really," explains Jimmy, "he killed them all with his own guns. Shot them dead. One he even nailed in our own backyard!"

"Wow," I murmur.

"You know," Jimmy goes on, "maybe we can get one of his guns later and go hunting!"

I think about me, a gun, and a deer, and almost puke.

After we change our clothes, Jimmy shows me around the rest of the house. Plenty more pictures of a crucified Jesus decorate the walls.

"Your family seems to like Jesus," I say to Jimmy.

"He's our lord and savior," replies Jimmy, "and he died for our sins."

"Uh huh," I shrug, having no fucking clue what he's talking about, wondering why that Jesus guy never cut his hair.

We make our way to Jimmy's backyard where we play catch with a hardball and a couple of mitts.

"Are you having fun?" Jimmy asks.

"Sure," I answer.

"Wanna have even more fun?" he then asks.

I tell him, "Sure, whatever."

Jimmy puts down his mitt, tells me to do the same, and then motions for me to follow him into his garage.

I do.

We enter the musty room, where the first thing I see is an old red pick-up truck.

"We don't park it outside," explains Jimmy while pointing at the truck, "because dad says it makes us look lower-class."

I nod my head, again not knowing what the fuck he is talking about.

I follow Jimmy around the back of the truck and he tells me to look on the flatbed. Before I do, I smell something really sweet. And awful.

"What's that smell?" I ask him.

"Just look in the back of the truck, George," explains Jimmy.

I do.

Then, I puke.

Hard.

It was a dead deer. A huge dead deer, with blood all over its side and flies buzzing around its head.

It's just laying there, looking at me with that same blank

expression, dried blood around its nose.

"My dad killed it a few days ago. Maybe tonight he'll let us help him cut it up!" Jimmy exclaims, ending the staring contest between myself and the dead animal.

So I puke.

Again.

"Are you okay?" asks Jimmy Foster.

I tell him that I am, it must be bad cafeteria food. Those nasty cafeteria ladies must have wiped their butts on the hamburger buns, and blown snot into the vanilla pudding.

"That's why I let my mom pack me lunches everyday," Jimmy replies. "Today I had a rabbit sandwich!"

After wiping the rest of the vomit off my chin, I follow Jimmy into his dad's workshop. There he begins nailing two pieces of wood together. Making a cross. About one foot wide and one foot high.

"Whatcha doin'?" I ask my fifth grade friend.

"Making a cross like Jesus died on," he tells me.

"What for?" I ask, "To scare off vampires?"

"Vampires?" says Jimmy Foster, confused.

"Don't you watch *Creature Features* or *Chiller Theater*?" I ask.

"What's that?" he asks in all seriousness. Every kid I know watches those horror movie shows.

"TV shows," I explain to Jimmy.

"My dad and mom don't let me watch television very much," he tells me, "only stuff about God. And hunting."

"Oh," is all I can say.

*

About fifteen minutes later I find myself in Jimmy's backyard with one wooden cross, and a Daisy Rifle BB gun. It is around five in the afternoon, and the sun is getting ready to set. It will be dark soon.

"I guess we could always use the cross and gun to protect ourselves from the undead," I joke.

Jimmy just stares at me blankly. Like his father's dead deers.

"We have to find a frog," Jimmy then explains.

"Okay," I say, "but why?"

"For the cross," says Jimmy.

It makes no sense to me, but I help Jimmy search around his backyard, front yard, and little pond until we find one. A big one. A bull frog.

"Wow," says Jimmy, as he holds the writhing green reptile in his right hand, "this frog is perfect."

"Okay," I say, clueless, "what do we do next?"

"Now we pray," says Jimmy.

Jimmy then closes his eyes, while holding the frog, and says a bunch of religious stuff, none of which I have ever heard before. Some of it is even in a different language. Regular Latin, I guess, not the Pig kind.

When he is through, he opens his eyes.

"Sorry I didn't join in," I say, "all I know is 'God is great, God is good, thank you God, for our food.'"

Jimmy smiles and pets the frog.

"Now what?" I ask, wondering what in the hell is going on.

"Now it's the frog's time," he says.

Jimmy takes a small hammer out of his back pocket along with three nails he'd taken from his dad's workshop. He then grabs one of the frog's front legs, and nails it to the cross. He then does the same to the other. Blood pours out from each hole in the frog.

"What the fuck are you doing?" I scream at my friend.

Jimmy, very calm, answers. "God's work."

Jimmy then pulls the frog's hind legs down really hard, and nails both legs together, to the homemade crucifix.

The frog now bears more than a passing resemblance to all the Jesus pictures scattered around the Foster household.

"It's still alive," I say, feeling queasy.

"It has to be," Jimmy explains, "for the sacrifice."

He then plants the cross, with the frog on it, firmly into the dirt.

"Jimmy . . . ," I say.

"Not now George," says Jimmy.

I look at his face. Tears are rolling down his cheeks.

"We must send this frog to heaven, from which it came," says Jimmy, "we must offer it to our lord, Jesus Christ."

Jimmy then motions for me to follow him. I do. We walk about ten or fifteen paces away from the crucified frog.

"I had to pull it's skin real tight," explains Jimmy, as he loads up his BB gun, "it works better that way."

"What way?" I ask, as I look at my friend, the gun, the Jesus frog, and the tears rolling down Jimmy's face.

"This way," he says as he pumps his BB gun a couple of times, then takes aim at the frog, and fires.

Suddenly the frog explodes. I mean, its insides fly all over the place. Some stringy stuff lands in my hair. I think it is frog intestines.

"The tighter the skin, the faster it dies," explains Jimmy, as he pulls the crucifix out of the ground. All that is left on it is some wet green skin.

I puke for the third time that day.

*

The Foster dining room is much like the Foster living room,

except there are only eight deer heads, and one bobcat head.

"So Jimmy tells me you two are best friends," says Mr. Foster, as we sit at his family's dinner table.

"Um, yeah," I say, looking into the dead eyes hanging above us.

"George is my pal," explains Jimmy.

"That's so nice," says Mrs. Foster.

Jimmy's sisters, both of them, laugh.

"You two shut up," says Mr. Foster to his daughters. "Jimmy finally has a friend."

"So George," says Mr. Foster, "what does your dad do?"

"Um, I dunno," I tell him. I really don't. All I knew at that point in my life was that he wore a suit and worked in Manhattan.

"Well," says Mr. Foster, "I'm sure he has a good job. It's expensive to live here in Greenwich."

I nod my head like I know what he's talking about.

"And you know something else about Greenwich?" he asks.

I shrug my shoulders.

"This town keeps the filthy Jews out if it. Jews are the reason this country is going down the toilet, straight to hell."

I look at the heads hanging on the wall, and wonder just how long it will be before mine is up there, joining them.

"Jews," explains Mr. Foster, "are put here on Earth by the devil. They are here to take all our money and steal our souls. Jews are fucking evil. They are antichrists."

"Jonathan, please," says Mrs. Foster.

"Please what?" he yells at his wife, "let me tell you, George, Jews own everything, and run everything. Ask your father. He's a smart man, living here in Greenwich, away from those dirty kikes."

"Yeah, dirty kikes," repeats Jimmy.

I say nothing. I'm afraid anything I say will sound Jewish. So I look up at all the dead heads.

"I shot them all myself," Mr. Foster explains proudly. "In fact, tonight we are having venison. Here, try some."

Mr. Foster puts some bloody deer meat on my plate. Then he continues with the other children's and his wife's plates. Jimmy eats some. As do his sisters. And mother.

"You're not a little pussy who is afraid to eat deer, are you?" Mr. Foster asks in his very deep voice.

"No way," I say, and put some on my fork, slowly bringing it to my mouth.

"Good," says Mr. Foster, "because the meat on your plate is from that buck right there." Mr. Foster points to the deer head directly above mine.

"We just thawed him out yesterday," Mrs. Foster explains.

I look at the meat and put some in my mouth, looking into the eyes of the dead animal above me.

"Yup," says Mr. Foster, "shot it, skinned it, and gutted it myself."

I feel myself gag, and run to the bathroom to puke for the fourth time that day. As I'm puking, I notice a picture of Jesus above the toilet.

*

The night only gets worse. Jimmy and I camp out in his back-yard for a while with a pair of loaded shotguns. Jimmy tells me deer often visit, and we can kill them if we see them. He also tells me about the Antichrist, and at my prodding, about how evil Jews are.

"They're the scum of the earth," he tells me.

Finally I break down and tell him the truth.

"I'm a Jew."

"Okay," he eventually says, "but don't tell my dad. He likes you. I would hate it if he beat you up."

The next morning at breakfast Mr. Foster is the first to speak.

"I heard a shot go off last night, did you boys nail a buck?"

Jimmy tells him we saw a deer, and that I had shot at it and missed, therefore scaring it away. What Jimmy didn't know was that I had missed it on purpose.

"That's too bad," says Mr. Foster, "that feeling you get after your first kill is amazing."

"Umm," I reply.

"Really," says Mr. Foster. "You get an incredible rush. You feel that with your own hands you can actually take a life. The power is incredible. It's like being God."

"I'll remember that, sir," I say.

*

Right after breakfast, I explain to Jimmy and his parents that I have to go home. Right away.

"But it's Saturday," Mrs. Foster complains. "You and Jimmy should go play in the woods or something."

I tell them that while I would really like to, I have chores to do. Lawns that need mowing, stalls that need cleaning, and cars that need washing. What I don't tell them is that never have I looked so forward to doing chores.

"You're a very responsible young man," Mrs. Foster replies. "Your father must be very proud of you."

I just shrug my shoulders.

"Well, I am," says Mr. Foster, and with that gives me a big hug.

"Thank you for being my son's friend," he then says.

"Yes," Mrs. Foster echoes. "Thank you."

With that, Jimmy and I walk to the front of his house where

my bike is parked.

"Thanks for coming over, George," Jimmy says, as he goes to shake my hand.

"You're welcome," I say, and grab his overly firm hand to shake it back.

*

As I tuck my jeans into my socks so they won't get caught in the bicycle's chain, Jimmy asks if I can come over again next Friday after school. I should have told him that I couldn't, that it was Shabbat. But not knowing shit about being a Jew, all I could say was that I'd ask my parents.

Which, of course, I never did.

EVERY OTHER SUNDAY

"COOL!" EXCLAIMS LUKE, AS HIS spit splashes on the forehead of some balding old guy who is staring up at us.

Actually, lots of people are staring up at us.

Including my mom, and Nick, who look terrified. Even from our viewpoint, which is over a hundred feet above them.

We are on the Thunderbolt roller-coaster at Coney Island. Only there is no thunder. Or bolting. In fact, we are motionless. Well, at least our little train is. Luke and I are having the time of our lives. People wave at us, and we wave back. We are also busy spitting on people's heads and giggling, yelling things to Sam on the ground as he yells back.

As I look around at the dozen or so other passengers on the ride, I begin to feel their tension. Of course, this doesn't bother Luke or me.

So what if the ride is stuck over a hundred feet up in the air?

So what if the only thing that separates us from certain death is one thin metal rail which we swear we hear creaking?

So what if we hear fire engines coming our way as tears begin to roll down my mother's face?

It has only been about forty-five minutes and we aren't really in a hurry to get anywhere. That is, until, I feel the legendary Nathan's hot dogs and french fries I'd eaten hours earlier start to make their way south. Fast.

"What's wrong, George?" asks Luke as I clutch my stomach.

"I gotta go," I moan to my brother.

"Number one or two?" he asks, seeming genuinely concerned.

"Two," I manage to eke out.

That's when Luke begins to laugh his head off.

That's also when our cart slides on the thin metal track a few feet, then derails.

Then, suddenly, everyone is screaming.

But let me back up a bit.

*

Pretty soon after my parents' divorce, Luke, Samuel, and I find ourselves in a Connecticut court somewhere upstate. On the way there, Lester and Cybil stop at a McDonald's and let us order anything thing we want. Luke has a double cheeseburger and Sam, two hamburgers. Me? I have two double hamburgers. Which I am able to eat in two bites. One bite per burger.

That is one thing I am proud of, being able to stuff all that food into one tiny mouth and not choke to death.

Anyway, as we sit gulping down our food my father and step-mother make it quite clear what we are to say in court.

"When the judge asks how often you want to see your mother," my father explains, "you tell him as little as possible."

"But I like her," exclaims Sam, who is all of three or four years old.

"That's not the point," Cybil explains. "When you see her you are putting your life in danger."

"Yeah," Lester continues, "she's a good-for-nothing junkie who will have you selling your bodies on the street in no time."

Of course, I don't know what "junkie" means, but it doesn't sound good. As for the "selling our bodies" part, I can't imagine anyone wanting to purchase a toe, finger, or even an eye, unless they were building Frankenstein monsters, for which I thought they robbed graves.

Who knew?

"She'll also leave you alone with Nicky," Cybil adds, trying to scare us.

Nicky, of course, is Nick, my mom's new husband, and according to Lester, Judas himself.

Turns out Nick and my dad were best friends until Nick, or "Nicky" as they call him, "stole" my mom away. Of course I later found out from Nick that this wasn't true. He and my dad had only met two or three times, hardly enough time to become "best friends."

So my dad and stepmother command us to tell the judge we really don't like our mother, but we are reluctant.

"Do you ever want to eat at McDonald's again?" my dad asks us.

We tell him of course we do.

"Then do what I say and you'll eat at McDonald's all the time!" he promises.

Of course, he lied.

*

After seeing the judge we are told we can continue Sunday visitations with my mom and Nick, as we've been doing. Except now, only on every other Sunday. Of course I feel cheated. I can't even imagine what my mom and Nick will feel. There are fifty-two weeks in the year, meaning fifty-two Sundays. We can only see my mom every *other* Sunday—which means only twenty-six days a year.

Boy, did we look forward to our Sundays.

We'd go on mini-adventures, which, in our minds, were as intricate as exploring the wilds of Africa, climbing Mount Everest and even exploring outer space. Each and every one of those Sundays we'd wake up around seven in the morning and try to make time fly until my mom and Nick arrived in what we called the "Batmobile," an old car with big fins and bright tail-lights. Later it turned into a big, bad yellow Cadillac.

We'd wait on our half-mile long driveway, called Juniper Hill for some reason, doing all sorts of things to pass time, from making ramps and jumping our bikes over them, to playing with G.I. Joe and Captain Action dolls.

Captain Action.

He was my favorite.

He had costumes for Spiderman, Superman, and even the Phantom and the Lone Ranger.

One doll—many suits.

The toy industry learned from this mistake pretty quickly, I guess, as Captain Action was only on the market a few short years.

Also, if it was winter, and there was snow, which there always seemed to be, we'd sled down our neighbor Mrs. Mackenzie's hill. Sam had this cool orange sled called an SPV (Snow Powered Vehicle), and I had a blue bathtub-looking thing. Luke, of course, had the classic Arrow.

As we sled down the small hill which was a mountain to us, we would stand up on our sleds and ride over the "jump" (a small rock sticking out of a small pond), trying to remain on our feet. Sometimes we did this lying down. When we weren't tackling the "jump," of course, we were tackling each other. We called it "snow wars."

If it was summer and the grass on our fourteen acres of land had risen above an inch, "hippie grass" according to my dad, we'd be cutting that until my mom arrived. Or at least we would *look* like we were cutting it. We'd push the manual mower around while my father, stepmother, or tattletale sisters watched. When their eyes weren't on us, we'd dump the mower and whack yellow jackets with sticks.

We also liked to jump from the stone wall of our back porch and pretend we were parachuting into war. Or pretend James Bond just shot us and we'd fall off the mountain side and die.

Finally, at almost ten sharp each and every other Sunday, my mom and Nick would pull up in their big car and we'd go on an adventure, leaving my father, stepmother, and sisters to ride around on horses. Of course we'd have to clean their stalls when we got home.

*

Every other Sunday we'd have a different adventure, but it would always start at a small candy store on Putnam Avenue in Cos Cob, right next to the barber shop and across the street from a shack that later became Crazy Taco.

My mom and Nick would take us into the place and tell us to pick out what we wanted, candy-wise, for the day. We grabbed bags of M&Ms, Sugar Babies, and Milk Duds. My mom would always take a Charleston Chew, and Nick, a box of violet gum. The old guy, Lou, who worked in the store, would tell us how lucky we had it with nice parents like these and we'd smile.

Of course, when we went in there on other days, with Lester and Cybil, we'd shield our eyes and hope like hell we weren't noticed. When we were it was always difficult to explain that we had two sets of parents. It was the late sixties and divorce wasn't that common, especially in Greenwich.

Sometimes my mom and Nick would take us someplace local to eat. We'd beg them to take us to Stamford, at least, but they'd just laugh and call us silly. Sometimes we'd see people we knew. We had to wonder what they were thinking. Were we kidnapped? Why were we with these strange adults? Where was Lester, our father? And Cybil, our mother?

Actually, it was Cybil's idea for us to call her "mom," and to call my mother "Barbara." It was also Cybil's idea for us to never mention our real mother, or Nick, to the outside world. We soon learned if we did mention them we got nothing to eat and were slapped around. My mom didn't seem to mind being called "Barbara," her name, but a few times she did hint at having us call her "mom." When Cybil heard about it she told us it would just confuse us, and besides, heroin addicts liked to be called by their first name.

We had no clue what she was talking about, but she did have a mighty big wooden spoon that hurt like fuck.

So, after the candy store, where I'd also stock up on Marvel Comics, while Luke went for Archie, and Sam, Richie Rich, we'd be on our way to the day's adventure. Sometimes it was as simple as driving golf balls or playing mini-golf, and seeing a movie. Sometimes it was a long trip to Great Adventure or Palisades Park, where we'd go on plenty of rides and stuff our faces with cotton candy; never mind the M&Ms we'd feed to the monkeys and ostriches at Great Adventure. And sometimes we'd just go to Barbara and Nick's apartment in Brooklyn.

I liked those days the best.

We'd arrive at their place on Ocean Avenue and my mom would immediately put a bunch of Charleston Chews in the freezer. Later we'd crack the long candy bars into little pieces and eat the chocolate, vanilla and strawberry chunks until our stomachs hurt. My mom would sometimes have fresh peas in their pods in her refrigerator and I'd fill up on those as well.

Luke and Sam would always complain when we got to the apartment. "There's nothing to do," they'd whine, "Let's go do something!"

But I was happy there. I would pretend that I lived there, in the little closet by the front door, the only space not filled with books or Nick's art or my mom's hairspray. I imagined that I went to school nearby, and the other kids wouldn't beat me up all the time for being a Jew. Some of them were Jews as well.

I'd also imagine calling Nick "Daddy" and my mom "Mommy."

Sometimes it would even slip out of my mouth by accident. I'd get all embarrassed but my mom and Nick would just play it off like nothing happened.

They ruled.

*

One of the things I loved doing at my mom's place in Brooklyn was going into the basement with Nick. Whether it was to play hide-and-go-seek, catch (with a rubber ball), or to shoot his BB gun, it didn't matter; it was all fun.

Okay, I lied. I liked the BB gun the best. It looked like a real police-issue revolver, and the tiny gold balls that shot from the thing stung like a son-of-a-bitch. We'd shoot cans full of holes, bottles into tiny pieces, and paper targets Nick bought at sporting good stores. I got to be a really good shot after some practice. So good that my brothers gave up on the BB gun they once fought over.

Nick was amazed that I always got bullseyes, but I wasn't. In my mind that paper target across the room wasn't really a paper target, it was something else. Or someone else.

*

On the days we went to Brooklyn, we'd usually end up at a movie or Coney Island due to Luke and Sam's insistent bitching. And sometimes mine, too.

We once went and saw a James Bond double feature, *Diamonds Are Forever* and *You Only Live Twice*. During both movies we sat in the balcony and Luke kept standing up, trying to peer down the actress's low-cut dresses or bikinis. Nick and my mom thought it was cute. I just wondered if he actually got to see anything.

Another day we took my mother's father, Grampa Sam, and his wife, Vivian, to see the *Kentucky Fried Movie*.

The ads on TV promised it was good silly fun for the whole family.

After the movie started, we found out it wasn't. Naked boobies, Catholic high school girls in trouble, drug references, and a full on fucking scene at the end. My Grampa Sam pretended to sleep throughout the entire film while Vivian just cackled and cackled. When it was time to leave I was afraid to stand up. From the look of Luke, him too. It was tent city. Finally I pretended to spill some soda on my lap just to cool things down.

On the way home, we had a nice, awkward silence. All except for Samuel, who kept asking why that woman in the movie took off her clothes and climbed on top of the man while the news anchors watched.

While seeing movies rocked, Coney Island ruled.

Besides all the cool rides, there were the go-carts. The signs said you had to be at least fourteen years old, but good old Saint Nick took care of that. At ten he had us whipping around the rubber-tire surrounded track in the large steel fenced off area just east of the Cyclone. We'd tear ass as fast as we could, Nick right along with us. After a while, the guy who ran it would stop and Nick would pay for us again, and again, and again. Luke was, by far, the fastest in the family. For some reason, he always got a car that beat Sam and me by miles. Actually, Luke was probably fast because he just didn't care. If he crashed, which he often did, he'd just get up, wipe off the blood from his hands, elbows, or face, and haul ass some more. Sam and I, on the other hand, played it safe, except when we were mad at each other, then it was Death Race 2000 time.

Another great attraction at Coney Island was the Hellhole, a ride, which until it crashed into itself and collapsed, killing a few people, was still in existence. Luke and I loved that ride.

But not the first time.

From the looks of it, we thought it was a spook-house, and that's why Nick and my mom got us tickets. Of course, the sign said we had to be at least sixteen to ride, but, again, Nick took care of that.

There was also a sign which read "$1 dollar to watch." My mom paid for Sam and her, while Nick, Luke and myself entered the attraction.

Once inside, it was clear this was no spook house. We then entered a round room covered with thin, wooden panels.

"What the fuck is this?" asked Luke, always the one with the potty mouth.

"Shit if I know, motherfucker," I replied.

"Hi George and Luke," we both heard Sam say as we looked up and saw him and my mom looking at us standing in the barrel.

"I got a bad feeling about this," Nick said as I saw that worried look in my mom's eyes.

Suddenly the room starts to spin. And I hadn't even touched a bottle of wine.

Faster and faster.

The next thing we knew, all three of us find ourselves pinned up against the wooden wall. Trapped.

Then it happened.

The floor beneath our feet slowly dropped out of sight and we found ourselves floating on the wall. We also heard my mom screaming from above.

Of course, then I puked.

But an amazing thing happened. The vomit didn't go down like gravity demanded. Instead, it clung to my face and the wall right next to my face. Like a blob. Luke laughed like crazy as he turned himself sideways. Nick just held his stomach, waiting for it all to end. Finally, after what seemed like hours, but in reality was no more than a minute or two, the floor slowly rose and we slowly fell. The vomit slowly moved as well.

When it was all over, I think I was crying.

But that didn't stop me from bragging about having ridden the thing the next day in school. Later, I grew to really love that hell hole.

*

The Wonder Wheel, probably the most famous ride at Coney Island, also had an age minimum. Nick took us on that, too, but he forgot to mention the part about the swinging carts.

So Luke, Sam and I screamed our brains out the first time we rode it, and every time thereafter. We loved it.

But we loved the Cyclone—Coney Island's ratty wooden roller-coaster that feels like it will fall apart at any moment—even more. The thing would violently shake, rattle, and roll, and you'd be thrown around like a rag doll, kinda like being at home in Greenwich, only fun.

And then there was the Thunderbolt, in the Astroland section of Coney Island. Standing over a hundred feet high, it was painted an obnoxiously bright blue and red and spiraled like an old telephone cord. It had turns on it where you'd almost be upside down and went so fast there was no way my mom would ever let us on it, no matter how much Nick begged her.

One day, she relented.

And we got to ride it, for the first and last time.

While we were in line waiting to strap ourselves into the tiny carts all hitched together, Sam begged my mom to let him on as well.

"No Sam," she told him, "It's bad enough I'm letting your brothers go."

Sam begged and pleaded but she stood firm.

Good for her. Sam would have cried the minute the thing moved.

So there we were, Luke and I, going up the first giant incline on the Thunderbolt, when we heard the tracks start to creak.

"This can't be good," I said to my little brother.

"I know," he replied. "It's *great*!"

Once we reached the top of the ride it just stopped. Dead.

"Why aren't we moving?" Luke demanded to know, speed freak that he was.

"I dunno," I said.

Luke's question was then echoed by everyone else in our line of carts. As people slowly began to panic, I looked down and saw my mom, who had a very worried look in her eyes. I also looked out at the ocean which, at that time, seemed almost swimmable. I remembered how on lots of every-other-Sundays my mom and

Nick would take us deep-sea fishing off of Sheepshead Bay; we'd play poker with the other fisherman and always take their money.

Perhaps, all that was now over.

There we were stuck high up on one thin creaking rail.

It was then I thought about my mortality. On an every-other-Sunday.

*

My mom and Nick let us do some crazy shit on those special days. Sometimes they let us drive their car around supermarket parking lots at full speed. Sometimes when it was hot, but most of the time when there was lots of ice.

We liked that.

On some days we got to shoot the BB gun. And when Nick or my mom wasn't looking, we shot it at one another.

Then there were the days we'd go body-surfing at Jones Beach. The waves stood very tall against our tiny bodies and Nick would teach us how to swim forward really fast just as we'd feel the wave break. He always warned us about the undertow, which, of course, Sam called "the under-toad."

We loved those days, and the ones when Nick would play the "great white whale" at some indoor Holiday Inn swimming pool, where we tried to hang on to him underwater while he violently attempted to shake us off.

Not that violently, I guess, since we always seemed to hang on.

Then there were the times we'd see movies in the South Bronx, Harlem, or sleazy Times Square. The screen would be torn somewhere, and usually rows of seats were knocked over or, worse, just really sticky. The audiences screamed a lot more than we were used to in Greenwich, but they also seemed to have a lot more fun, even if they sometimes did have little fights with silly objects like brass knuckles and pointy knives.

We were kids. We didn't care. And when we were with Barbara and Nick, nothing bad ever happened.

Just weird. Like the old lady in that 42nd Street basement who put four swords down her throat, then asked us if we wanted to try. Or hanging out with their gay friend, Bruce, who had a little statue in his house of a man putting his penis inside of another man, who had his penis inside of a dog. Nick explained it away as "gay humor."

We didn't think it was funny, but it sure was hilarious the way Bruce talked like the girls we knew in school. Later, when my mom and Nick moved to West Fourth Street in Greenwich Village, we found out lots of people talked like Bruce. By then we called everyone who lived there "clones" because they all looked exactly alike.

But nothing like the Thunderbolt had every happened to us.

Until now.

*

"Cool!" exclaims Luke, as his spit splashes on the forehead of some balding old guy who is staring up at us.

I look down at my Mom from the top of the Thunderbolt and she looks pale. Much more than usual.

"I gotta go," I moan to my brother.

"Number one or two?" he asks, seeming genuinely concerned.

"Two," I manage to eke out.

That's when Luke begins to laugh his head off.

That's also when our cart slides on the thin metal track a few feet, then derails.

At this point my mom is crying, and Nick doesn't look too good, either. Of course Sam thinks that this is the coolest thing he's ever seen, and continues to wave and yell up to us. We wave back, trying not to let him know we are actually scared shitfull.

Then we hear the fire engines.

And the megaphone.

"Attention Thunderbolt riders," says a loud voice from behind a large bullhorn held by a Brooklyn cop in full uniform. "Please stay where you are."

Like we are going anywhere.

"Try not to move around at all," the cop continues, "as the ride is now unstable."

"Unstable?" Luke repeats.

The only thing I notice that's unstable is my stomach. Well, to be honest, my butt.

I am prairie-doggin' and praying they will get us the fuck down before I have an accident.

Finally the fire engines arrive, and the guys with the big hoses that girls love start to make their way toward us on one of those cherry-picker things, only it doesn't reach up far enough.

"We're so fucked," Luke finally says, realizing the real danger we are in.

I just nod and hold my butt tightly shut.

"Attention Thunderbolt riders," begins the cop once again, "we are going to attempt to send another Thunderbolt cart on the tracks to push you back on the rail."

I look down at my mom in utter fear. By this time, she is crying on Nick's shoulder. Nick looks like he is about to cry as well.

Meanwhile, Sam just keeps waving and shouting, "Hi George and Luke!"

We watch in total terror as an empty train full of carts makes its way up the steep incline behind us.

"We're so dead," mutters Luke.

Everyone else is screaming. Even the guy in the last cart with the Fu-Manchu mustache and black leather vest.

Then it hits us.

The empty train, that is.

Hard.

Luke and I are jolted forward and all of a sudden we find ourselves going down the first hill. Too fast. It feels like we are in free-fall and this is the end. At the bottom, the carts turn sideways and stop. About six feet above the ground. It takes the cops and fire-fighters about ten minutes to get us all out.

As soon as Luke and I get off the fire-truck, my mom and Nick run toward us with open arms, and we run toward them.

By this point I had shit my pants, but it wasn't very much, and as it made its way slowly down my left leg the warmth somehow embraced me.

Then my mom and Nick do as well.

Sam too. Although I'm sure he doesn't know why.

"Never again," sobs my mom as she begins to suffocate us. "Never again!"

Nick tells my mom he agrees "100 percent" and that he'll never allow us to go on a dangerous adult ride ever again.

"You promise?" cries my mom. "You really promise?"

"I certainly do," says Nick, wiping the tears from his warm brown eyes. And he keeps his promise, too, for about two whole months.

Then the first loop-de-loop opened at Six Flags Great Adventure.

KLAUS CONTROL

SO THERE I AM, WITH this fucking migraine headache which makes me want to puke, sharpening the edge of the ax, making sure it will split a hair, or a head, in half. I load up my Crossman 760 rifle with lead pellets and strap on various hunting knives, box cutters, and even a couple of hammers. Around my forehead, I knot the putrid paisley tie my dumb-ass dad gave me for my birthday. A tie he claimed was passed down through generations of Tabbs, but still had a tag-sale sticker on it for one dollar.

I look like Rambo, junior.

As I continue spinning the antique sharpeners' cement wheel, by peddling the machine with my feet, my legs grow sore. Sparks fly everywhere as I imagine what I'll do to the guy once he comes up our driveway.

I'll fucking take the knives and gut him. I'll wear his intestines around my neck like a feather boa. I'll take the hammers and, like John Henry, hammer in the morning, hammer in the evening, and hammer all over his fucking face. And with the rifle, I'll shoot so many holes in the bully's body he'll leak when he drinks a glass of water.

As for the ax? I'll raise it above my head, look into his eyes, and delight in his fear. Fear and hatred.

For me.

Because I am a Jew. And if there is one thing he told me he hated, it was Jews. As the ax pierces the air toward his head, I'll see a glimmer of hope for mercy in the dark blue pools of his eyes. But it will be too late. The ax, unstoppable, will slice through the top of his skull, into his brain, and end this drawn out battle once and for all.

I imagine him falling to the ground, ax in head, knives in chest, bullet holes in body, and I laugh.

Laugh until the police arrive.

But let me back up a bit . . .

*

Finally I'd had it with Joe Klaus. Since early in grade school, he and his sister, Katy, beat the hell out of my brothers and I on the school bus on a daily basis. Along with the rest of the brat pack.

Most of the time I stood up for my brothers, and took the beatings originally aimed at Luke and Sam. Of course they would watch, helpless and terrified. Besides being the only Jews, we were also the only runts of the bus, the smallest for our ages.

Joe and Katy's little brother, Ken, would sometimes join in. While Joe or Katy's fists flew in a frenzy, Ken would hop on my chest and stamp on my head or groin. Meanwhile, the other kids cheered him on.

It may as well have been a Roman Coliseum.

And, ironically, I may as well have been a Christian.

*

One afternoon, towards the end of the school year, while Joe and Katy are tap dancing on my face to a song on the bus driver's radio, I bit Katy so hard I end up with a lump of flesh in my mouth. Katy screamed in pain and jumped off of me, holding her now bloodied ankle. Ken saw the damage done to his sister, then kicks me so hard in the mouth I spat out two teeth.

"You're gonna pay for what you did to my sister, Jew," Joe said to me as he punches and kicks me so hard in the chest I can't breathe.

"You little fuck," he continues, "I'm gonna make you wish you were never born, faggot!."

"Fah you," is all I could manage to reply.

"You say something, Kike?" Joe asks as he bitch-slaps me around some more.

Suddenly I am puzzled; I've never heard that word before.

But it sounds like "kite," so I wonder what in the fuck it has to do with me?

"Tabb," Joe Klaus yells, snapping me out of my thoughts. "You are so dead that you're dead." Clever guy that bully is.

"I'm gonna come to your house at four o'clock and kill you," Klaus continues, "and if your brothers are around, I'll kill them too."

And he means it.

He then climbs off of me and goes to comfort his sister, who is now holding her bleeding ankle with two hands to stop the blood. I sit up, spit out some more blood, but still have the taste of fresh flesh in my mouth.

We arrive at our bus-stop at a quarter to three, and my brothers run to our house as quickly as they can. By the time I arrive home, Luke and Sam have changed into their play clothes and bolted to friends' houses.

I don't blame them.

I think about doing the same thing.

But I know if it isn't today, it'll be tomorrow.

Or the next day. Or the next.

It is time to get this over with.

As I think about the possibility of my own demise, the scent of flowers, cut grass, and dog shit seep into my nostrils. I'll miss those smells.

I'll miss the rest of my life.

*

I enter my house through the kitchen via the back porch and happen upon my stepsisters who stayed home that day, as well as my stepmother, Cybil. Also with them is our housekeeper, Attie, and her little yapping poodle, Peachie.

As I make my way past them I notice puzzled looks on the children's faces, and a smile on Cybil's. Attie just looks pissed.

I go to my room where Attie quickly follows.

She's been working for my father since I was three, and is the only caring adult living in the Tabb residence. Attie quickly puts ice wrapped in a towel over my eye and another one over my mouth. She tells me that fighting is a bad thing but she understands that sometimes it is necessary. She continues to hold the ice to my face and soon some of the swelling goes down. I tell her I am feeling better and need to rest. She tells me she understands and leaves.

As soon as she is out the door, I quickly change into my "play clothes," which consist of a "Keep on Truckin" T-shirt, ripped jeans, and a pair of fake Chuck Taylors with holes in the bottoms that I'd purchased myself at Woolworth on Greenwich Avenue. I take my Crossman 760 out of the closet, and load it with pellets that I had filled with solder a few weeks earlier. I heard they did more damage that way. I then pump the gun a couple of times and fire it at a photo of Cybil and Lester taken in Thailand.

Bullseye.

I get Cybil right in the kisser.

Then I glance over at the clock. A quarter till four. It's almost time. So I quickly run downstairs to the basement where I search frantically for the right tools to do the job.

Joe Klaus is on his way over to kill me.

And I'm not about to let that happen.

I find a bunch of knives hanging in my dad's workshop along with tool belts. I strap on the belts, and hang the blades from the tiny leather hooks. I find an ax, and sharpen it on an old stone wheel Cybil had purchased at a local auction. I then find the hammers and hang those from the belt as well. For the coup-de-grace, I take a tie my dad had given me for my birthday, which I'd been using to clean my gun, and tie it around my head. I am ready for that fuck-face, Joe Klaus.

I look at the clock hanging in my dad's workshop and see that it is three minutes till four. Any minute now I will hear Klaus peddling up the driveway on his ten-speed. My heart begins beating very quickly, and suddenly I am drenched in sweat. As the second hand on the clock passes the one-minute-to-four mark, I finally hear his voice outside of the house.

"Tabb," yells Klaus. "Come out of your Jew-house and face me like a man."

My heart races even faster.

"Come out now," he continues, "or I'm coming in for ya."

I start to open the basement door, but freeze. I try to move, but can't.

I am scared.

I feel like I am in one of those dreams where, no matter how fast I run, I don't go anywhere. Only this is real.

So I think about Klaus. How he and his little brother and

sister kicked my ass and my brother's as well. I also think about how my dad did the same thing and how Cybil eggs him on and then tells me that I deserve it. I think about my own mortality, and realize for the first time I don't give a shit.

Suddenly I'm able to move my arms. Then my legs. I find myself opening the basement door and walking out into the bright sunlight. Shielding my eyes, I see Klaus on his ten-speed about thirty feet away from me on the black-tarred driveway. He is staring at me, the shiny knives hanging from the belts, the ax on my hip, and gun in my hand.

He says nothing, and I say the same.

We look in each other's eyes, and if this was a movie, you'd hear the theme from *The Good, the Bad, and the Ugly.*

"Ready to die, Tabb?" shouts Klaus, with the slightest quiver in his voice.

With my best Clint Eastwood imitation, I tell him I am.

"Then I'm coming for you, Jew," he screams as he rides towards me. "Prepare to die!"

I pump the Crossman 760 a couple more times and take aim at Joe Klaus's head using my right arm. With my left, I take the ax from my hip and prepare to cut him down.

As Joe Klaus pedals closer, I feel my trigger finger start to itch. It is time to scratch it, and Klaus.

When Joe gets less than ten feet away a huge shadow suddenly blocks me from the sun and Klaus's head. It quickly yanks the gun from my right arm.

I look up and see Attie, our housekeeper.

"George Tabb," she yells, "just what the hell do you think you're doing?"

Shocked, I am speechless.

I think Klaus is, too.

"You think you are gonna shoot this boy?" she continues to scream. "You think you gonna chop off his little chicken neck with that big ol' ax?"

Again, I am speechless.

"Well, George Tabb," she says, always using my last name when she was super angry, "you just better think again. You get your skinny little behind back in that house, put away your father's tools before he finds out you took them, and I'll deal here with this Klaus boy."

"Umm," I just stammer.

"George Tabb," she continues, "you best shut your mouth and get inside, or I'm gonna whup your behind so bad you'll be walking around like a duck for a month."

"What you waiting for?" she yells a half second later.

I say nothing and go into the basement. Well, I pretend to anyway. Actually, I hide behind a stone wall, and listen to what Attie is yelling at Klaus. I also peek out every once in a while.

"What in the hell do you think you're doing, Klaus boy?," Attie yells at the little shit. Before he can answer, she continues. "You think picking on children younger than you is a good thing? Fun? How'd you like it if I was to slap you upside the head?"

And with that remark, she does.

"You like that?" she yells, then does it again.

I hear Joe Klaus start to sniffle.

"You best be riding your ass back to your house now," Attie tells the bully, "and if you was to ever pick on my boys again, a slap upside the head ain't the only thing you gonna get. Remember that, Joe Klaus."

At this point he begins to cry.

"Go home now, Joe Klaus, and don't let me catch you back here," says our hero housekeeper, "and you tell Betty that she better keep a better eye on your ass. You understand?"

Joe Klaus nods his head.

"Good," says Attie, as she slaps him one more time.

Joe Klaus rides his bike away, sobbing. Attie then makes her way toward the basement and catches me peeking.

"You saw the whole thing, didn't you, George Tabb?," Attie demands.

I nod my head.

"Well, I don't think none of them children are gonna be picking on you again," she says.

She then explains to me that she and Betty, the Klaus's housekeeper, once had it out in Harlem years earlier, because of a man they were both seeing.

Attie tells me she beat Betty so badly she was in the hospital for a week.

Stunned, I just thank her.

"You're welcome," she replies. "Now get your bony ass upstairs and wash up. I need some help fixing dinner."

So I do.

After that day, I helped Attie fix lots of dinners.

*

The next morning on the bus, there is a strange silence. I look around, see Katy with a huge bandage on her ankle, while Joe and Ken sit brooding. They say nothing to my brothers and me as we take our seats. It must puzzle the hell out of the other kids. We ride in silence to school and every once in a while I catch one of the Klauses just staring at us. Simmering.

Finally, as the bus pulls into the Parkway Elementary School driveway, all the kids stand up, as usual, even though Jackie the bus driver yells for them to sit down. Jackie parks the bus and then all the kids run out for another fun day of learning to read and write and hate one another.

As Joe, Katy, and Ken depart from the bus I almost feel bad for them.

Maybe their home life isn't wonderful and taking out their frustrations on others helps them feel better. Perhaps they are good kids underneath all the mean-spirited bullshit. Maybe they just need some love, and some kind words of encouragement.

So I walk up and tell them something I think they need to hear, something I've been dying to say since I boarded the school bus that morning.

"My maid can beat up yours!" I brag.

And for once their big mouths stay shut.

ROY TWIG

So, THERE I AM, IN FRONT of the whole damn camp.

Me and Roy Twig.

And everyone is yelling stuff at us like *retard* and *faggot*.

And the counselors, of course, are doing nothing. They just watch.

Suddenly, one kid runs up and punches Roy right in the face, and then snarls, "we don't want your kind here, you fucking retard. Go back to the institution."

Most campers laugh, as do some of the counselors.

"Hey George, you fucking pussy," some kid screams from the back of the lynch mob, "why are you sticking up for a retard? You some kinda fag?"

I'm at a loss for words.

I mean, fuck, I *am* wearing shorts.

Then I feel my face get hit.

Hard.

My nose starts to bleed as one of the counselors yells at the kids that we'd had quite enough, but the campers don't think so. The insults keep getting hurled at us, and Roy just looks at me, confused.

Then some little snot yells that his parents didn't want him going to camp with a retard. I yell back to him that Roy is my friend, and a good person. But the kid just laughs, as do many of the others. Then the same turd walks up to me and tells me to get the fuck out of his way.

His name is Brian.

He's a huge Irish kid, and one of the worst bullies at Camp Kabian.

I tell him, no, I won't move, and to leave Roy Twig alone.

Then Roy says to me in a quivering voice, "George, why are they doing this? Where's my ball? I want my ball."

The ball Roy is referring to is a ball he has made out of masking tape, and had somehow become very attached to.

The kids continue laughing as Brian warns me for the last time to step out of his way. I look at the counselors who passively watch, and suddenly realize that there is no way they are going to stop this.

Roy Twig, a retarded kid, is about to be beaten to a pulp. And the counselors probably want it to happen. They are tired of having to take care of a retarded boy. They probably figure if he gets beat up, then he'll leave, and he's no longer their problem. So I bet they are excited to see Roy eat some fist.

Only thing is, there's one thing they don't count on.

Me.

Motherfuckers.

*

I think it is my twelfth summer. My parents had decided that it would be a good thing for me to leave Greenwich for the summer and go somewhere away.

Far away.

Like New Hampshire. Lake Winnipesaukee to be exact, to a camp called Kabian, some Indian name meaning some shit about land and rivers and trees and all that crap. I don't care. The important thing is that I will be getting out of my house and away from my father and stepmother.

When they ship me away to camp Kabian, they tell me that they'll come visit on parents' weekend. Five weeks away. So, of course, I look forward to that weekend like a hole in the head.

I'm off to camp with my trunk and my army-issue duffel bag and everything else. The bus ride is very long from New York City, so I get to talk to lots of kids. One of them is Tony.

Tony Gordon.

He was born in New York, too.

A slightly overweight kid, he tells me on the way to Kabian that his parents want him to lose weight and that this camp promised to help with that problem.

I think, "What *problem*?"

We arrive at camp, and as luck would have it, Tony and I are bunking in the same cabin. By cabin, I mean *cabin*. The kind you build with Lincoln Logs. The one on the sticker of maple syrup bottles.

There are lots of them. It seems the whole place is overrun with cabins. And they are out in the woods, in the splendor of nature, with bees buzzing and birds chirping, and all that shit. And it is totally fucking weird.

There is electricity, so we do have lights.

Still, we are in the middle of some mountains, there is no heat and, at night, it gets fucking freezing.

But I am a man.

I can take it.

Besides, it is great to be away from my parents, two stepsisters and one half-sister, as well as my brothers. The only people I miss are my mom and step-dad. But we keep in touch through many, many letters.

Of course, in these letters, I ask for "care packages" and get lots of good stuff. Like *Mad* magazines, candy, and whatever else a kid would want while away at summer camp.

My father and step-bitch send me packages as well. In those I find my dad's old socks and T-shirts to keep me warm, rips and all, as well as books on math and English, so I will be ready for school the following year.

Actually, my dad does send me a picture of him and Cybil in Mexico or some other third world country where he could be King. In the picture he was holding up a giant fish he had caught. In the letter that accompanies the picture, he tells me to put the picture up in my cabin, near my bunk, so I won't miss him.

Of course it ends up in the outhouse, with the rest of my shit.

The first couple of weeks go okay. I learn to swim in a mountain lake with temperatures that freeze my balls solid. Right across from us is Mount Washington, topped with snow, in the middle of the summer.

Also, I learn to whittle. That means getting to play with knives, which rules. I also learn how to get more food at the mess hall by eating very quickly, steer a canoe (some would argue that one), and about the joys of pissing out our cabin door while watching the steam rise along with the sun.

As the summer progresses, I grow closer to my friend Tony and our cabin counselor, Chris. Actually, our cabin is called the Tigers cabin. It's what we named ourselves. Other cabins have names like the Bears, or the Eagles. But we are the Tigers. Named after a dog on the *Brady Bunch*.

Chris grows to really like Tony and me and sometimes takes us into town with him and his hot-ass wife, Pam. She has the largest breasts of any woman I have ever seen.

Once, in the car on the way back from "town" (one gas station and a general store), I am really tired, and ask Chris and Pam if I can go lie down in the back of the station wagon. Pam then asks if I would rather lie on her lap. So that's where I wind up, with the best pillows I have ever felt. Through that euphoria, I sort of remember looking up from the back seat into the rearview mirror and seeing Chris staring at Pam and me. He has a funny look on his face. And a huge smile.

*

Everything is fine until the beginning of August.

That's when we get a new counselor, as well as a new camper.

The counselor is Brad, and he is a total and complete dickhead.

He wears his Kabian T-shirts tucked in like a puss and is some hot-shot tennis player. In fact, his job, besides being our caretaker, is teaching tennis. His sneakers are always white and he doesn't like any of the kids. He is always chatting up the female counselors and ignoring us.

One day, while swimming in Lake Witchestit, I get some water up my nose and begin to cough. I then get really dizzy and start to drown. I do my best to yell and wave at Brad for help, but can't get his attention. He is too busy talking to Eve.

The lifeguard.

Finally, she sees my fluttering arms and jumps in and saves me. When she drags me up on the beach and makes me cough out the water, I start to feel better. Then, as Eve walks away to get me a towel, Brad leans over and calls me a little asshole for ruining his chance to score with "the hot chick."

Nice.

*

The new camper is Roy.

Roy Twig.

The day he arrives we are told that a new camper will be joining us, and he that he is "special," meaning mentally retarded.

Brad tells us that it isn't fair Roy is coming to Kabian. He complains about the fact that Roy will be lodging in our cabin. He says that Roy is fourteen years old, a full two years older than any other Tiger, and will be quite a lot to handle.

He tells us to try and be nice to Roy, but not to worry if we aren't.

He says if Roy were to leave Kabian, it wouldn't be such a bad thing.

Then we all meet Roy Twig.

As he enters the cabin with his parents at his side, he seems like a very nice kid. He is about my size and weight, with a soup-bowl haircut, blonde hair, and the bluest eyes I've ever seen. He is wearing his camp issued Kabian shirt, and blue shorts. In his hand he has a ball made of masking tape.

As he plays with it, Brad's golden retriever, Buffy, keeps trying to take it away. After a while Roy begins to cry and murmurs "bad dog" and "mine." All the kids laugh, as does Brad. Roy's parents just kinda smile, uncomfortable.

Finally, I get up the nerve, and push Buffy away. Roy simply says "Thank you."

And then smiles.

A wonderful smile.

Pure and honest.

It makes me feel nice. All over.

So Roy and I become friends. We go boating together, swimming together, and even go on nature hikes together.

I like the kid.

Sure, he is a little slow, but everything in the world is new to him.

He likes the trees.

He likes Buffy.

He likes the mountains.

And the lakes.

And the food at the camp, which, I guess, does make him retarded.

Roy likes *everything*.

And *everyone*.

And that is a problem because the kids at Camp Kabian don't like Roy. Nor do most of the counselors. They all think he is weird—a freak with buck teeth, and spiky hair, who sometimes cries and screams.

This is very troubling to many.

Maybe they are scared of the something unknown about him.

Maybe by being near him, they think they'll become him.

Whatever the reason, it blows.

And me?

I just think he is another kid like me, who likes to have fun.

Hell, he likes to melt ants with a magnifying glass just like me. He likes to eat really fast so he can get more food. He hates the freezing cold water, and also believes that the outhouse smells worse than anything else in the world.

So what if he wets his bed every once in a while, and cries in his sleep. He is nice. A good kid. And everyone takes advantage of him.

*

It starts with a group of older campers telling Roy that they lost their candy in the outhouse, and wonder if Roy will please go get it for them. They lead him to the tiny shed and tell him the candy is down in the area where all the crap and piss lies.

So Roy dives in. He comes out covered with shit, and smells horrible.

But Roy just keeps apologizing for not finding their candy.

The other kids have a good laugh while Brad freaks out and calls him a "fucking retard."

And Roy?

He just cries.

Another time, we are playing softball, and the ball lands near a nest of wasps. None of the other kids will go retrieve the thing, so they send in Roy, who is just happy to be useful. He gets stung so badly he spends three days in the infirmary.

I still blame myself for not being around him that day.

One night, all the Tigers, as usual, are making fun of Roy just before bedtime. I beg them to stop for the umpteenth time, but they just call me "fag hag" and "retard lover." I look over to Brad, and he just smiles.

Anyway, the kids keep yelling at Roy and soon he starts to cry. A lot.

So I sit on his bed next to him and hug him. I tell him not to cry and that everything will be okay.

Of course I then become "his boyfriend."

So that night, after everyone, including Brad, is asleep, Roy and I decide we are going to run away. Where? I have no idea.

But Roy has to escape their torment—their constant calls of "retard" and constant reminders that their parents don't want them attending camp with him.

Somehow, I feel it is my job to protect him, like I would, with any other friend.

When I had told my father over the phone about my new friend, Roy, he told me that it was not my responsibility to take care of him and I should hang out with normal kids—even that fat kid, Tony. That he wanted me to grow up "normal."

So, Roy and I take off into the woods and sleep there that night. We build a campfire and light it with a book of matches I stole from Brad's trunk. None of that rubbing two sticks together bullshit. And that night, Roy opens up to me.

As much as he can, anyway.

He tells me that he loves me and his masking tape ball very much.

And Buffy, the dog, too.

And his parents.

And his sisters.

The list goes on.

As he speaks, I see a pureness in him I don't see in others, not even in myself, and for a minute, I am jealous.

Finally, the fire goes out and Roy and I fall asleep underneath a sheet of twinkling stars.

Of course we later wake up freezing our asses off and thankfully are found by a search party the next morning around five.

*

The next few days at Camp Kabian are hell. Everyone except Roy Twig yells at me and says that I took Roy's life into my own hands, that I should never have run away with a retarded kid and I'm a complete loser. I'm told that Roy is a bad influence on me and he'll be leaving the camp as soon as they can find some way to kick him out.

They also warn me not to hang out with him anymore, or they will tell my father.

I tell them to go right ahead.

*

Things continue to get worse and worse. Finally, a pure and simple hatred for Roy develops at Camp Kabian. The counselors hate him because they are responsible for him and the campers hate him because he is different. This leaves both Roy and me very confused.

And very alone.

Then one morning the shit hit the fan.

Roy was throwing his masking tape ball around and it somehow landed on Brian's bunk.

Brian, being the camp bully.

Buffy, Brad's dog, hops up on the bed and decides that besides her job as a retriever, she should also wet the bed. To help it grow. Only problem being, Brian was still in the bed.

Asleep.

Dreaming of beating up sheep, I'm sure.

Brian starts yelling and screaming at Buffy, and then aims his anger at Roy. Roy starts crying and runs outside—during reveille. The whole camp is lined up and the guy playing the bugle suddenly stops.

Brian emerges from his cabin yelling that Roy is a retard.

A *dead* retard.

The rest of the camp joins in, chanting "Roy the Retard is dead."

The counselors, of course, do nothing.

Brian then yells that we don't need his kind around here, just like in a bad western. He screams that Roy Twig belongs in an institution. Roy grows confused and just wants his masking tape ball back.

He then asks me why they are doing this. Why is *everyone* being mean to him?

I tell him I don't know.

Then some kid punches Roy in the face, and Roy just stands still for a few seconds with a strange look on his face.

A look I'll never forget—one of total confusion and utter disappointment.

Not just with us, but with everything.

Then Brian yells for me to get out of the way, that he is going to teach the retard a lesson he'll never forget.

I beg him to leave Roy alone. He warns me to get out of the way.

So I warn Brian to leave Roy alone.

While this is happening, the entire camp is watching. Then something weird happens. I start shaking.

Not just a little, but a lot.

I can't help it. I also feel my lips quivering, and feel tears running down my face. And then I start crying. Loudly.

Everyone just stares at me, shocked.

I am frightened myself. I don't know why I am crying or shaking, but I am.

So I look at Roy.

And he looks at me. With his big, beautiful blue eyes. And then says in a very soft voice, "Please don't cry, George."

And then I snap.

*

I begin to hit Brian with everything I have. Fists. Knees. Elbows. Whatever.

It takes four campers and a counselor to tear me off of that son-of-a-bitch.

By the time they do, I have given him two black eyes, a bloody nose, and a bloody mouth, minus a few teeth.

As they drag me away, I am still crying and shaking.

So Roy hugs me, and starts crying as well.

As we stand there, sobbing on each other's shoulders, we hardly hear the shouts of "fags," "homos," and "retards."

It doesn't mean anything anymore.

*

The following day Roy Twig is kicked out of Camp Kabian. They say he is too much trouble and too much responsibility. So his parents come and pick him up. They thank me for being such a good friend to him and tell me that Roy will never forget me.

Truth is, I'll never forget him.

PLAYING RIGHT FIELD

THE SOUND OF SPRINKLERS AND smell of freshly cut grass greeted my senses that summer every Saturday morning as I made my way out onto the baseball diamond which was exclusively for my Little League team, the Parkway Pirates. Well, not Little League, actually. More like Mini-League or Bush-League. I was in the fifth grade, my brother, Luke, in the fourth. We were the only Jewish members on the team.

It was my stupid idea to join the team in the first place. Maybe if my dad had played more catch with me in the backyard instead of dressing up like a woman under his business suits my yearning for big hard balls and stiff bats wouldn't have led me down the road to hardball hell. But, alas, it did.

That summer began as most others did for a Jewish kid living in Greenwich, Connecticut.

With relief.

I wouldn't have to ride the bus to school everyday where the kids would beat the shit out of me just for having a big nose and brown curly hair.

Instead I would get to stay home and play with my Captain Action, Dr. Evil, and G.I. Joe dolls, or pedal my Chopper bicycle, as my brother Luke raced his ten-speed up and down our driveway, while my youngest brother, Sam, tried keeping up on his Schwinn.

Or so I thought.

"Boys," my dad says to us about the third day into our freedom, "you have to get off your asses and do something this summer."

I protest, telling my father I am doing something. I'm making another Super-8 movie, and this one is going to be my best one yet. Better than "Flush," my last one, starring claymation creatures that escaped from my toilet.

Luke, also protesting, claims that this was the summer his two new gerbils were going to be launched into orbit. That he has built an Estes Rocket that takes four D-sized engines, and has padded the payload section with nonflammable material so this time his astronauts would survive and not end up like Timmy and Jimmy did—cat barbecue.

Sam, my future doctor brother, about to enter the third grade, says that this summer he's going to dissect all his stuffed animals, and "then put them back together again."

Last summer, he had just left them in pieces.

Dismembered. Especially Goofy. His pillow-like guts had been strewn across our backyard for days, until Barkwell, the golden retriever who lived next door, decided to eat what was left of the Disney character and then throw it up all over our front porch.

"That's not good enough," says my dad in his stern voice. "This summer I want you boys to learn the value of money."

I knew what was coming next. Jobs. Work. And there was no way I nor my brothers, would have any of that.

"We want to join the Parkway Pirates," I suddenly blurt out, surprising myself as much as my father, Luke, and Sam.

"You do?" asks my dad.

"We do?" asks my brothers.

"Yeah," I say. I explain how much we love the Yankees, which we do. So much so that when we go to games with my mom and Nick, we yell "Bozo" at Thurman Munson as much as possible. I explain to my father that baseball is the great American pastime (I'd read that in the World-Book Encyclopedia of 1972) and that since we were Americans, it was our duty to play the game.

"You guys play baseball?" asks my dad. "You little pussies won't even play touch football when Uncle Marty and Uncle Wuzzie come to visit."

"It's supposed to be 'touch'," I tell my dad.

"You and Uncle Marty jump on top of us," adds Sam.

"Yeah," echoes Luke.

"Do you guys know the first thing about baseball?" my dad then asks.

I tell him we do. That the Japanese baseball mitts he'd given us had been put to some use. We had played catch with one another at least twice and that Grampa Jack, his father, also played catch with us every once in a while, when he wasn't driving golf-balls and having us chase them.

"So that makes you good enough for a team?" asks my dad.

"It's the Parkway Pirates," I tell him, "they'll take anyone. It's not like it's a *real* team or anything. Just kids from school."

My father reluctantly agrees to let us play, but as it turns out, Sam is too young, so he is only allowed to watch. Which is good because of the whole T-shirt fiasco.

*

"You fucking little brats are going to have to join a car pool or something," my stepmother, Cybil, bitches at my brothers and me as she drops us off at Parkway Elementary School the first Saturday morning of baseball practice. "Either that, or ride your bikes. It's only eleven miles."

We just ignore her as we usually do and run out to where a bunch of kids are gathered and toss the ol' hardball around.

"Hiya guys," I exclaim, excited. I see some of my classmates, as well as others I'd seen around the hallways, cafeteria or boy's room.

"Oh look," says one kid with straight blonde hair and cold blue eyes, "it's the Jews!"

Everyone laughs except Luke, Sam, and I.

"I didn't know Jews played with baseballs," yells James Smith, a kid in my math class. "I thought they only played with Matzo Balls!"

More laughs.

"Hey Tabb," says Mike, another kid from one of my classes, "what kind of mitt is that? A *kite* mitt?"

I look down at my Japanese mitt and frown. It's huge, and flat like a kite. Someone had once told me it was a *pitcher's* mitt, but I couldn't tell from all the Japanese writing all over it. All I knew is that my dad got it *cheap*, which he loved to brag about.

Luke, on the other hand, had a real mitt. One with a hole in the back where you could stick out your fingers and everything. It had some name crossed out on the back of it with black magic marker, and "Tabb" written in, instead. I once asked him where he got it and he told me he'd won it from some kid in a bet involving getting the kid's sister naked.

That's my brother.

So all the kids start chanting "Jews, Jews, Jews, Jews!" over and over while Luke and I stand there with dumb looks on our faces, and Sam just sits in the grass and starts to pick it. Then eat it.

"That's enough," I suddenly hear a man's voice yell.

I turn around and see him.

Our coach.

Kurt.

And his girlfriend.

Dawn.

Who has the biggest breasts I'd ever seen. And I mean *seen*. Her halter-top barely contains her half-dollar sized nipples and her miniskirt appears to disappear.

All the kids get quiet.

"I'm Coach Andrews," says the guy with the sideburns all the way down each side of his neck and a curly blonde afro as wide as the Goodyear blimp.

All the kids stare at him.

"But you can call me Kurt," he says, with that million-dollar smile that twinkles and everything.

Some kids mumble "hello."

"And this is my girlfriend Dawn," adds Kurt. "She'll be helping me coach you guys this summer."

"A girl?" asks the blonde-haired blue-eyed nazi child.

"A girl," says Luke, with his tongue halfway to the ground and a tent growing in his shorts.

"Wow," is all I can mumble.

"And," adds Kurt, "for your information, I'm Jewish."

I should have guessed from the brotherly 'fro.

"So there will be no more name calling. Of any type. Got that?" Kurt informs the kids.

Most kids nod their heads and my frown about my mitt turns into a big smile. Finally, a guy who looks as old as my parents or teachers and doesn't call me a pussy, fag, or kike.

The rest of the first day of practice goes well, with Kurt hitting lots of balls out into the field where we all practice catching them and throwing them to either first or second base. I almost catch one, but when it hits my flat mitt, it hurts so bad I have to drop it. But, still, it's fun.

*

The following Saturday is our third day of practice. We are doing Tuesdays, Thursdays, and Saturdays. When we arrive, Cybil asks who owns the VW van with all the bright daises and peace signs painted all over it.

I explain to her that it is Coach Andrews's.

Kurt's.

"Fucking hippie," is all she can say before she again tells us that we'd better join a carpool or ride our bikes the eleven miles because she was a very busy woman.

Ignoring her, we run out of the car and greet Kurt.

"Hey Kurt," I say to our coach as I go over to his van, which is parked behind the fence near home base.

"Hey George," Kurt says back, then picks me up and gives me a big hug. He then does the same with Luke.

"How's it going guys?" he asks.

"Groovy," replies Luke.

"Groovy is far-out," says Dawn, Kurt's girlfriend, who today is wearing daises in her hair.

"Far-out," echoes Sam. He is with us again, just to watch us miss balls and strike out.

"Well," says Kurt, "why don't you guys make your way onto the field and practice some and I'll join you in a few minutes."

We tell Kurt we will and that we'll see him soon. He nods his head and gives us the two finger "peace" sign.

A few minutes later, after standing in the field and having no balls hit to me, on purpose, I make my way to the Volkswagen van to see what's keeping Kurt.

Turns out Dawn is.

I look into the side door, which is facing away from the dia-

mond and there is Kurt, kissing Dawn, with his hand fully surrounded by what appears to be a furry animal he's grasping
between Dawn's legs.

"A doggie!" I yell, shocking Kurt and Dawn.

Dawn quickly pulls down her skirt the inch or so it will move,
while Kurt looks at me with a strange look on his face.

"Do you know what we were doing?" he then asks me.

I tell him that they were kissing and that Dawn has a puppy
somewhere that I don't see anymore.

"Uh-huh," says Kurt then he pulls out a hand-rolled cigarette, shows it to me, and asks if I know what it is.

"A cigarette," I say.

"Groovy," says Kurt, then lights it up, inhales, and passes it to
Dawn.

They both pass it back and forth for a while, each inhaling it
quite deeply.

"My biology teacher, Mr. Williams, says that smoking is bad
for you," I tell the two adults.

"Uh-huh," says Kurt again, as he exhales a cloud of funny
smelling smoke.

"Far-out," adds Dawn.

Then Kurt puts the cigarette out and we both go to the field
to practice some baseball.

At the end of practice that day, Kurt tells each of us to bring
six dollars the following Tuesday. That he is getting us Parkway
Pirates T-shirts, with our last names on the back of them and
everything, and that we will wear them at our first game, which was
two weeks away.

*

That night, after my father gets home from work, Luke and I, very excited, tell our dad about the shirts over dinner.

"Six dollars?" my dad screams, "for a fucking T-shirt?"

"It has our name on it and everything," I say, very excited.

"Back when I was in school," my father explains, "our shirts cost a nickel,"

Of *course* they did.

"I want one, too," exclaims Sam, who has been going to practice with us the whole time and has sort of become the nonofficial cheering section for the Jews of the Parkway Pirates.

"Buy them yourselves," snaps my dad, "I don't work hard all day just to get ripped off. It's bad enough I have to pay for the food on this table!"

I feel my heart sink as I look at the canned asparagus, sweet potatoes with marshmallows on them, and barely cooked liver.

"Come on Lester," says Cybil, my step mom, in a move that is surprisingly decent of her, "get them the fucking shirts."

"Are you telling me what to do, woman?" screams my father, as his skin begins to turn purple and he starts to shake uncontrollably.

"Yes I am, you dick-head," she replies.

My dad, through his clenched teeth, tells her to shut the fuck up, and as he does so, all us kids clear out of the dining room, knowing a nasty storm is brewing.

Suddenly the dishes begin flying and the name-calling starts. Then the chairs, table and fists come next.

Another Saturday night at the Tabb residence.

*

The following Tuesday Luke and I show up with six dollars, between the both of us. As it turns out, my father gave into my stepmother.

Halfway.

It was decided that Luke and I would *share* a T-shirt since we both bore the same last name.

Tabb.

And since we both played right field because of our dismal catching abilities, we wouldn't be playing at the same time, anyway.

That was the logic.

I remember telling my dad that it wasn't fair and that I was going to ask my mom and Nick, my stepfather, for the money. He told me when he was a kid he loved to share things with his older brother.

Especially beds, when they went on "family vacations." He threatened that if I asked my mom or Nick, he'd make sure I didn't have working hands to play baseball with at all. And he was serious.

So, Luke and I give Kurt the six bucks and he asks where the rest of the money is. We then have to tell him our dad will only let us get one.

He laughs nervously, and then tells us that things will work out okay anyway.

Dawn, overhearing all this, exclaims, "Wow, your old man is sure a downer!"

Luke just nods his head and looks down at the ground.

"Don't feel so bad, honey," says Dawn and with that, picks up Luke and hugs him tight between her double-D boobies.

Luke just closes his eyes and smiles.

As do I.

The rest of that day and night I spend asking Luke over and over again what they feel like.

*

It's the first game for the Parkway Pirates and most of the kid's parents are there to watch. Of course, mine aren't. Cybil had dropped us off two hours earlier because she was going shopping in the city with my stepsisters and the choice was either go early, or ride our bikes the eleven miles.

Uphill.

My dad said he couldn't come see us play because he knew we'd be awful and he didn't want to be embarrassed in front of the other parents.

So it was just Luke, Sam, and I.

Sam, being our cheerleader, of course.

Since it was a home game, we were put out to pasture first.

"Okay Luke and George," says Kurt, "who wants to play right field first?" We had both chosen right field because, as everyone knows, the least balls get hit that away.

"I do!" I say, because I want to wear the purple Parkway Pirates T-shirt first. We had it still sealed in the plastic bag that Kurt and Dawn had given it to us in about an hour earlier.

"You'll stink it up," exclaims my brother. "I want to play first!"

"At least I take showers every day," I yell at Luke.

"I take showers too," says Sam, who is sitting by himself on the bleachers watching everything.

"You'll flip for it," is Kurt's answer as he throws a penny up in the air.

I call heads and lose.

Luke gets to wear the shirt first.

He takes off his dirty white Italian bread T-shirt and puts on the clean purple Parkway Pirates shirt with the letters T-A-B-B pasted up hugely on the upper-back. Sam and I are jealous, as we watch him run onto the field.

Three outs later, the top of the first is over and Luke takes off the shirt and gives it to me. We are at the end of the batting roster and know we won't be up this inning, so I take off my "Keep on Truckin'" shirt and wear that purple flag of honor for as long as I can.

As I put it on, even though it stinks of my brother's sweat from the hot June sun, I feel proud.

There I was, on a baseball team, just like my heroes, Thurman Munson, Catfish Hunter, and even that pussy Met, Tom Seaver, who was at the game watching because he lived near by.

The bottom of the first inning doesn't go by as quickly as I thought it would. Our guys kept getting on base and suddenly Kurt yells that I'm on deck.

To bat!

The guy in front of me makes a base hit and the next thing I know I'm up.

Luke is called to deck.

As I stare at the pitcher from Norwalk, I hear the catcher utter things like "Oh, you're the team Jew, gonna strike out for us?" and "Swing batter batter swing!"

I ignore him and wait for the right pitch. It happens three balls and two strikes later.

I hit a line drive to short-stop, which the guy misses and suddenly I find myself on first, having driven in one run.

I'm in shock.

So, I'm standing on first base, in my purple Parkway Pirates T-shirt with the letters T-A-B-B proudly displayed on the back, when I see my brother walking toward home plate, in his dirty white Italian bread shirt.

I start to get that sinking feeling again.

Suddenly, Kurt runs out to me and tells me to take off my shirt and give it to my brother. I look at the crowd, then Luke, who already has his shirt off and is standing near home plate, waiting, and topless.

So I take off the shirt and hand it to Kurt.

As Kurt runs over and gives it to Luke, who quickly puts it on, not only do all the kids on the Parkway Pirates and the Norwalk team laugh, but the parents do as well. I hear some kids yell that my parents must be the cheapest Jews, ever.

And I find myself silently nodding my head in agreement.

As Luke waits for the right pitch and misses two of them, I feel the sun bake the skin on my bare back. I motion for Kurt to come over by waving wildly at him, and he does.

"Can I wear my other shirt?" I ask him, feeling silly standing on first base half-naked.

"Sorry George," says Kurt, "it's either a Parkway Pirate shirt or nothing at all."

I tell him that's okay and as he walks away I start to feel tears of embarrassment run down my cheek.

"What's the matter, fag?" asks the first baseman.

"Shut up," I say to the kid.

Two bad pitches are thrown to Luke, while Kurt and Dawn, acting as our surrogate parents, yell "Good eye! Good eye!"

"What's the matter," whispers the first baseman to me as I try and take a little bit of a lead, "your parents know you're a homo and have given up on you?"

I punch the little fucker in the face with an uppercut as hard as I can. He bites off part of his tongue and suddenly there's blood, everywhere.

Everyone is running onto the field in my direction.

Then they all tackle me.

The next thing I know every fist and foot in Greenwich, Connecticut, is making contact with my body. I look up and see my own team in purple Parkway Pirate T-shirts hitting and kicking the living shit out of me. I also see kids from Norwalk doing the same thing.

I even see some parents standing around. Clapping.

Finally, Kurt, Dawn, Sam, and Luke manage to pull me free from the crowd-gone-wild. I'm beet red and bruised all over and my nose and mouth are bleeding heavily. The umpire walks up to me, sees if I'm okay, then tells me I'm out of the game.

Luke complains to the umpire that it isn't fair and he's thrown out, too. So it turns out Sam gets to wear that Parkway Pirates shirt for the next eight innings. And as he does so, he keeps telling us that if we could fight every game, he could always wear it.

*

The rest of the summer spent with the Parkway Pirates, well, sucked.

Kurt keeps us out of as many games as he can, at our request, so we won't have to be embarrassed by having to change the shirt back and forth between the two of us. Eventually Cybil makes good on her threats and we find ourselves riding our bikes twenty-two miles three times a week to baseball practice. My dad never does make it to a single game and when I ask him for a new mitt because the Japanese one hurts when a ball hits it, he hits me.

But not everything goes badly.

Luke, Sam, and I grow to be really good friends with Kurt and Dawn. They let us sit in their painted VW van before and after practice, and listen to music they like from Hendrix to Cream to Three Dog Night, while they smoke their hand-rolled cigarettes.

Luke and I always stare at Dawn's breasts, which she was nice enough to flash at us every once in a while.

Then, at the last game, Dawn made my brothers and I brownies that were really, *really* good.

It's funny, but all I can remember about that day is laughing and laughing with my brothers and Kurt and Dawn, and wishing the summer I had wanted to end soon wouldn't.

But it did. And when the next summer rolled around, that prized Parkway Pirate T-shirt with T-A-B-B printed in huge letters on the back was nothing more than a dust rag and small towel to dry off wet dogs.

A tattered memory, like the previous summer.

THE FARM UPSTATE

"YOUR DOG BIT ME," CRIES John Shepard, as he covers his face with his left hand.

"Very funny," I say to my new friend, who had just moved to town because his father was an ambassador to some Middle Eastern country, but quit to join the "private sector."

Whatever that meant.

I was never really good at understanding what my friends' parents did for work. And when it came to my own. I was almost totally in the dark.

Some local kids had parents in politics, while others had parents who owned Fortune 500 companies.

And then, of course, there were the professional athletes.

As for politics, all I knew was that I got beaten up in school for wearing a McGovern pin my mom and Nick had given to me, that some family called the Kennedys were pretty much locals, and that the president liked to play golf around town.

As for Fortune 500 companies—I must admit I found it strange that so many people made so much money either predicting people's futures, or racing cars around a track like in Indianapolis. I wasn't sure which.

As for the athletes, them I understood. Especially Dave Kingman, who was on the suck-ass Mets, but played hockey with us every once in a while.

Anyway, I ask John to remove his left hand from his face so I can see this supposed dog bite.

He does and I almost faint.

My grade school pal had a rip in his forehead that reached from one side to the other. And it was starting to flap around, like our school flag when it was windy.

"Holy shit," I say to John, whose tears are mixing with blood, staining his white Izod shirt.

"He bit me!" John cries once more.

I look at him and am at a loss for words.

Suddenly, Attie, our house keeper, shows up on the back-porch where we had been busy taping fire-crackers to gliders and watching them blow up in mid-air.

"We gotta get you to the hospital," screams Attie, looking at John Shepard.

"Umm," I just stammer.

"Don't just stand there George Tabb," Attie says to me. "Go inside and get Cybil, we gotta go. Now!"

On the way to the hospital my stepmother keeps repeating that it must have been my friend's fault. That he "provoked" him.

Him being Thor.

Our Great Dane.

She also bitches about John's blood getting all over her car and that Lester should buy her a Mercedes Benz for being married to him, and having to take care of his three worthless sons.

All I can do is cry along with my friend, John. Whose face was slowing falling off.

It sucks.

*

We got Thor and Sassafras when they were just twelve weeks old. They were both tiny brown and black Great Danes, just like Scooby Doo.

Anyway, my brothers, sisters and I love those dogs. We had just lost Hennesy, our ancient Saint Bernard, and were happy to have two new wagging tails in the house.

When my father first brought them home, he told us kids that they were our responsibility and that we had to feed them and take care of them. Of course, we were more than happy to do so.

Well, feed them, anyway.

As they grew older, they grew bigger. A lot bigger.

Now, at a year old, Thor stands around seven feet tall, and Sassy, well she's about six and a half feet.

Together, they probably weigh more than four of us kids.

And eat about as much, too.

My father purchased a large garbage can which he keeps in the furnace room, next to the darkroom he never uses. In the garbage can is Kibble, pounds and pounds of it.

Mice, too, who also eat the kibble.

We hated having to get their food because mice would always jump out of the can once we opened it and wind up pooping on our heads in fear.

At first, we didn't know it was poop. It *looked* and *tasted* like bird seed.

But when we show it to our carpenter one day, while he's hitting golf balls in our back yard with his shirt off, he tells us it's mouse shit.

Cybil, while sipping from a glass of lemonade, laughs.

"Your kids aren't so bright," the carpenter says to Cybil, who's wearing a drawstring bikini with the top untied, sitting in a lawn chair, watching her favorite man. Topless.

"They aren't mine," explains Cybil, "how many times do I have to tell you that!"

"Oh yeah," says the carpenter-turned-PGA pro, "just the girls. Hey, George, go chase that ball and get if for me, huh?"

Later that day the carpenter asks me to show him exactly where the mice are. I do but we can't find any, so I build a trap out of scrap wood to catch one, alive.

The next day I do, with the help of some fishing line and a piece of cheese. I show the mouse to the woodcutter.

"Fucking little piece of piss," he says as he holds it up between his thumb and index finger. "I'll teach it not to shit on you."

He then takes out a lighter and ignites its tail. It runs around the kitchen, on fire and squealing, before finding an open window, and leaping to the front yard, where it continues to burn and sets fire to piles of leaves I just raked together.

When the carpenter sees tears in my eyes for the small animal, he laughs and calls me a pussy.

Cybil laughs as well, and then asks the carpenter for his lighter. Puzzled because she doesn't smoke, he hands it to her. She runs up to my room and grabs my favorite stuffed animal.

A lamb.

Named Cybil. After her.

Soft and white with holes punched in its ears for no reason.

She brings it down to the kitchen and lights it on fire.

Then laughs wickedly.

I cry as she tosses the toy out the window.

"Little pussies," comments Cybil. "Just like their father."

The carpenter laughs in agreement, then they both retire to my parents bedroom.

Sassy walks in, sees my tears and dries them with her tongue.

*

When the dogs are about a year and a half, my father buys us a tiny pony cart we can harness to Thor and Sassy. It's meant for Shetland ponies, but works fine with our oversized canines. Thor and Sassy pull us up and down the driveway and we even have races. One kid in the cart, the other riding a Great Dane bareback. It's lots of fun and we only get hurt about every other time.

As time goes on, I grow a lot closer to the dogs. Especially Sassy.

Thor's an okay dog, but not having his balls cut off makes him a little more than dominant. He continuously tries to hump the couch, the car, and the horses. Cybil remarks one day that she's insulted he hasn't gone for her.

Eventually Thor and Sassy do what dogs do and we get puppies. They're awfully cute and it's sad we have to sell them off. It's also sad that one is stillborn. Sadder still, when my dad hands me a shovel and tells me to put it with the rest of our past animals.

So I bury it next to Dead Eye Dick.

Our ex-cat.

Who was lucky enough not to be thrown into our pond in a burlap sack, alive, or let go in the woods about fifteen miles away by my dad.

Anyway, with the puppies gone Thor goes a little crazy. He keeps going into the laundry room, between the kitchen and the playroom, where Sassy once lay with their puppies. He sniffs around continuously, and starts to get a sad look on his face.

Sassy, meanwhile, doesn't really seem to care much, probably happy that the little ones aren't sucking on her eight nipples anymore.

Then the day comes when Thor loses it and bites my pal, John.

Once we reach the hospital, John gets a zillion stitches, and my father is told by Mr. Shepard that Thor must go. My dad thinks about it, then instead of getting rid of the dog, he chains him to a boulder in our backyard.

*

"Don't go near him," I tell Mike and Donald, my two best pals. "He bites!"

My friends don't listen and approach Thor with their hands held out, face up.

They slowly approach the giant and find him to be gentle.

And licky.

He licks their faces, their hands, and whatever else he can.

Donald and Mike laugh with glee, and I pet the dog as well.

"Why's he attached to this huge rock?" asks Donald, as he barely holds up the thick steel chain.

"Like I said, he bites," I tell him.

Both kids say he isn't biting now and I agree. I tell them what happened with John Shepard and they both say that Thor is a nice doggie and that John Shepard can sometimes be mean.

I agree, and explain I don't really know *what* happened.

Just that there was lots of blood.

"Cool," say Donald and Mike, together.

When my father gets home from work that night, Cybil tells him that my friends and I were taunting Thor. Before kicking my ass, my dad yells that Thor is chained to a rock for a reason. That he's dangerous, but he's not sure what to do with him.

One black eye later, I'm outside in the cool autumn air having Thor lick the tears from my face. Sassy, out for a walk by herself, sees us and joins in on the licking.

I tell the two dogs I love them and wish they were my parents.

They lick me in agreement.

*

Thor remains chained to that rock for months. Winter comes and Thor sleeps in the garage, but spends his days in the snow, near the rock.

I feel terrible for him.

But it doesn't stop me from playing hockey next door on my neighbor Andy's pond.

I like the sport. You get to wear huge-ass gloves and a helmet, so that when a puck hits you in the head it doesn't hurt. Same with the other kids' fists.

One day, while playing in sneakers, a kid named Kevin from down the street punches me in the face for no good reason.

With my nose bleeding, I ask him what he did that for.

"Cause you're a Jew," he replies.

I sigh and continue on with the game, trying to stay away from the kid.

The next day, the same thing happens.

And the next.

Finally, I wise up and bring Sassy with me to the hockey games on Andy's pond.

The first day, Kevin sees the overly huge dog and says, "What's the matter you dirty Jew, you need a dog to protect you?"

I tell him I do and so what?

The kid punches me in the face and tells me he isn't afraid of my "kike dog."

He changes his tune about thirty seconds later when Sassy is holding his throat between her teeth.

"Please Tabb," cries the bully, "I won't do it again."

I tell Sassy to let him go but she won't.

"Tabb," yells Kevin, "get her off of me, please!"

I ask Sassy once more to let the bully go. She does, but not before letting go of his neck and barking as loud as she can in his face.

Kevin leaves the pond that day, crying, and never returns.

For some reason, none of the other kids playing hockey ever body-check or stick me again.

*

As winter fades to spring, I get very busy with Cub Scouts and almost forget about the chained canine in my backyard.

That is, until, he bites my half-sister, Stephanie.

She's all of four, and forgets that her mommy told her that Thor is a *bad* doggie.

So she walks up to him to give him part of her cookie and, instead, he eats part of her face.

Cybil blames me when Stephanie gets bit because I was supposed to be watching her. And I was. Until she called me in to empty the dishwasher.

On the way to the hospital, Stephanie drips blood everywhere.

And Cybil decides she wants a driver to go along with her Mercedes from my dad.

I just hold my baby sister's cheek to her face, so it won't fall off.

*

A week later my father tells us that he found a really nice farm upstate for Thor. A farm where he will have many other dogs to play with, as well as other animals, where he won't be a threat to children.

The next day when I come home from school, he's gone.

*

Years later, I'm talking to my stepsister, Diane, on the phone. We are having a conversation about all our animals, and we remember Thor. I tell her that I just read a book where a father tells his kid that their dog also went to a *farm upstate*.

But, in reality, they put him to sleep.

Diane, not believing me, calls Cybil and finds out the truth.

Tearfully, we both realize that Thor didn't live out the rest of his life chasing animals around and playing gleefully with other dogs—he got the needle.

And for the first and last time in my life, I actually appreciate my father's deception.

BLIND BULLY BOY

I COULD FEEL THE PUKE make its way up the back of my throat filling my entire mouth. Creole spaghetti, burnt toast, and chocolate pudding is all I could taste as it began to leak out between my lips and seep between my fingers, which were covering my mouth.

"What's wrong Tabb?" asks Jimmy Foster, as he continues to pull the dead squid apart and lick the hard shell embedded inside, which reeks of formaldehyde.

I feel the bile juices drip down my chin as I furiously try to swallow.

"If you don't like seafood, there's always the sheep's eyes," says Jimmy.

With that remark, he takes one of the detached blue eyeballs that's lying on a metal plate before us and puts it in his mouth.

Then he bites down.

Hard.

Sheep-eye juice sprays all over my face, and the next thing I know, I'm running as fast as I can toward the boys' bathroom at Parkway Elementary School in Greenwich, Connecticut.

"Are you okay?" asks Mrs. Cole, the kindly old librarian, as I tear past her, chocolate pudding dripping off my neck and onto my red and white striped Izod shirt.

I say nothing and finally reach the restroom. There, I throw up my entire hot lunch, which cost around seventy cents. A lot of money in those days.

Afterwards, I go to the mirror, and begin the task of wiping the vomit off my face, neck, and my neighbor's hand-me-down shirt. Also the sheep-eye juice, which smells like vodka and raw hamburger meat.

As I continue to clean myself up, I hear someone open the boys' room door and I look in the mirror behind me.

I freeze.

It was him.

Bobby Kessler.

The kid who was making my fifth grade experience more of a nightmare than Jimmy Foster and his incredibly strange eating habits.

"Who's dat?" asks Bobby as he stares at me with his eyeless sockets.

I say nothing, and continue to wash myself off. I don't want a conversation with this kid.

"I know someone is in here with me," says Bobby, as he grinds one of his thumbs into his dark black empty right eye socket.

"It's me," I say to Bobby, perhaps feeling a bit sad for the blind kid.

Big mistake.

"Me who?" asks Bobby, as he moves toward me and the sound of running water.

"Me," I repeat, not wanting to tell him who I am. It's bad enough my younger brothers, Luke and Sam, have trouble with this kid, but it's worse with me. Because I am older than him, and should be able to defend myself.

"Tabb?" says Bobby, "Is that you?"

I say nothing.

"I think it is," explains Bobby, and with that, moves in and feels up my face. I don't mean he just touches it. I mean, he *feels* it up. Like I wanted to do with a certain big-breasted sixth grader.

First he touches my curly brown hair, then he puts his smelly hand with empty eye socket goo on my forehead, eyes, nose, and finally mouth.

"Let's see," says Bobby, "curly hair and a big nose."

I know what's coming next.

"I feel a Jew! It must be George Tabb!" he exclaims.

I try to move away, but Bobby backs me into a corner between the sink and a toilet stall.

"And I hate Jews!" continues Bobby.

The next thing I see is Bobby's left hand moving very quickly, then I feel a really sharp pain on the top of my head. I put my hand on the pain, and, of course, there is plenty of blood.

"You fucking asshole," I yell at the blind kid.

"Ha," is the only thing Bobby Kessler says as he leaves me alone in the boys' room with not only vomit on my Izod shirt but, now, blood.

Later, in the nurse's office, I have the same conversation I'd had a week earlier—one that I am bound to have again.

"How did this happen?" asks the old nurse as she sponges up my blood with lots of cotton balls.

"The same as last time," I tell her.

"You shouldn't make up stories," she says to me, cruelly.

"I'm not!" I exclaim. "It happened just like last time!"

"And I'm supposed to believe you?" she asks.

"Yes," I tell her, even though I know she won't.

And I'm right.

*

It wasn't like I had anything against Bobby Kessler. In fact, I remember the first day I saw him at school. It was during recess, right after the first block of lunch, which, for some ungodly reason, was at 10:45 A.M.

I saw him walking around the playground near the monkey bars, with his cane.

"Hey Tabb," said my then friend/enemy, Scott Applegren, "look at that freak!"

I never knew if I liked Scott or not. One day he'd be my best pal, telling me all about the joys of small animal torture and what girls actually hid in their underwear, but the next day he'd be like the other kids calling me "Big Nose" and putting his leg out in front of me so when I fell he could say "have a nice trip, see ya next fall!"

So I look at the kid Scott is pointing at. It's Bobby Kessler.

At first, I must admit, he scares the shit out of me. The kid has black holes where his eyes should be, and big brownish-black circles that extend over his eyebrows. He looks like a zombie.

"He's in fourth grade," explains Scott Applegren, "and I hear he's blind!"

I tell Scott that I can see that.

"But he can't!" yells Scott, then rolls around on the ground, laughing.

I tell Scott maybe we should make friends with him, and Scott, for some reason, thinks that's a good idea.

We approach Bobby Kessler, and his blind kid's cane, and I clear my throat.

"Hi," I manage to squeak out in my prepubescent voice, "I'm George, and I'm here with my friend Scott."

"You sound like a girl," Bobby Kessler says to me.

Scott laughs.

"Anyway," I say, "I would just like to welcome you to our school and maybe we can be friends."

"Friends?" asks Bobby, "You want to be friends? I'm not being a friend to a gay-fag with a girlie voice!"

"I think I like this kid," says Scott, and the next thing I know he and Bobby Kessler are laughing it up together and making up names for me like "Georgina," "Georgette," and of course, "Pussy."

A couple weeks later I'm called to the principal's office. For what, I've no clue. I hadn't done anything wrong that I was aware of, except for impersonating a punching bag for some of the bullies at recess.

I walk into the principal's office, and seated in the small and musty room is my brother, Sam.

"Hey Sam," I say to my youngest brother. "What's up?"

"I'll tell you what's up, says Dr. Perkins, the head of our school. "What's up is your brother has an attitude problem, and maybe you can help."

I ask what's going on, and Dr. Perkins explains that Sam was caught fighting with the new blind kid, Bobby Kessler.

"So?" I say, not liking that blind fuck very much, either.

"What the *hell* is wrong with you Tabbs?" yells Dr. Perkins. "The kid is *blind*!"

"He's a bully," says Sam, "and he started it."

I start to tell Dr. Perkins I agree, and that Bobby called me a girl, when suddenly the principal goes off the deep end.

"Bobby Kessler is the sweetest kid in this school. He would never pick on anybody," he yells. "You Tabbs are just bad news. Picking on handicapped children. What's next? Teresa Johnson? She's in a wheelchair! Perfect for you guys!"

Sam and I both start to say that this is unfair, but we're cut off.

"If I hear anymore of this," Dr. Perkins says, "you guys are gonna be suspended."

Sam and I stop talking. We knew that being suspended was bad. Not because we got to miss school, but because we'd have to stay home with our stepmother, Cybil, who was likely to kick our asses because she couldn't then hide in her bedroom with the carpenter, making all those funny noises.

*

That night Sam and I are discussing Bobby Kessler, when Luke walks into the room.

"You guys talking about that ol' thumbs-in-the-eyes Bobby?" he asks.

We tell him we are and explain what had happened to us.

"Bobby can be a real dick," Luke tells us, "a real cocksucker. A real whore-licking ball buster. A motherfucker and a cunt!"

Sam and I look at Luke like he's speaking another language, which, to us, he is. "He started a fight with me in the library today," says Sam, the third grader. "He called me a faz and a homamexicall, and hit me!"

"That's *fag* and *homosexual*," says Luke, the adult word expert, then asks, "Was it with his right hand or left?"

Sam thinks for a minute then says it was the right hand.

"Good," says Luke, "you really got to watch out for his left!"

When we ask him what he's talking about, he tells us to ask him another time. He's busy. The next thing we know, Luke is climbing out his second story bedroom window, and sneaking off to smoke cigarettes, read porno, and whatever else he does with his good friend, Norman.

About a week and a half later, I run into Sam in the hallways between fifth and sixth block. He's limping.

"What happened?" I ask him.

"Bobby Kessler," he replies.

"Did he kick you?" I ask, feeling anger well up inside of me, and wanting to kick the blind fuck's ass.

"No," says Sam.

Then he tells me what had happened.

And about the left hand.

I must admit, I almost didn't believe him.

Almost.

But two days later, the truth hits me.

*

It happened in the computer room. When I was alone with him. Mr. O'Neil, our teacher who, at the time, was teaching us "basic," had left the room because of an urgent phone call. There were supposed to be two other students in the class that day, the Shores, but as they were twins, they both had the chicken pox.

So it was me and Bobby.

Alone.

"Your brother Sam is dickless," Bobby tells me when the coast is clear.

I ignore him, hoping he'll vanish like his eyesight.

"All you Tabbs are fags," Bobby Kessler says. "In fact, you're Jewish Fags. Matzo-eating cocksuckers."

I tell Bobby to shut up, and warn him that Mr. O'Neil will be back any minute.

"That's enough time to kick your ass," he replies, and hits me in the face with his right hand.

Hard.

At first I'm in shock. A blind kid just hit me.

I'm not sure what to do next. If I hit him back I'd be more of a creep than I already was.

"What's the matter Tabb," yells Bobby, as I run around behind him, so he can't feel me with his outstretched arms, "scared of a blind boy?"

I tell him I'm not, and not to hit me again, or I'll tell Mr. O'Neil.

"Well then tell him about this," says Bobby Kessler, as he raises his left hand.

The one he just used to pick up his heavy-as-hell braille typewriter.

Bobby hits me on the head with it so hard, the next thing I know I'm sitting on the floor with blood pouring out of the top of my head.

"Ow," I scream, beginning to cry.

"Baby," snarls Bobby, as Mr. O'Neil strolls back into the classroom.

"My God! What happened to your head, George?" yells Mr. O, as he looks at my bloody head.

I tell him.

"Don't make up lies," scorns my teacher, "you were probably doing something stupid like balancing on a chair or table. Go to the nurse's office, and stop lying," he demands.

I tell him I'm not lying.

Then suddenly Bobby starts crying.

"George was scaring me," Bobby whines, now trembling, with no tears falling from his eye-less sockets.

"Get out of here *now* you little idiot!" yells Mr. O'Neil and, with that, pushes me out into the hall, where I make my way towards the nurse's office.

"His Braille machine?" asks the nurse in disbelief, a few minutes later.

"That thing is really heavy," I explain to her, tears drying up on my face.

"You know George," says the old nurse, "you really shouldn't make up stories about people. Especially special people like Bobby. It's not very nice."

I try to tell her that I'm telling the truth, but the more I explain the story, the more she begins to hate me. So I give up, get my head cleaned with alcohol and cotton balls, then make my way to my next class.

*

My next fight with Bobby is the day that Jimmy Foster eats the squid shell and sheep's eye in biology.

After I puke, and after he hits me with his damn Braille machine in the boy's bathroom, I again end up in the nurse's office, telling the same story.

"You really shouldn't lie," explains the nurse, "you can end up in Hades forever for that."

"What's Hades?" I ask her.

"Hell," she tells me in a mean voice. "A place where you'll probably end up."

I just nod my head.

"Bobby is a great kid," the nurse continues. "I can't believe you are jealous of him and make up stories."

I tell her I'm not, then she pours rubbing alcohol on my open wound.

I yelp in pain.

"Did that hurt?" asks the nurse.

Again I nod my head.

"Good," she says.

*

I make the mistake of telling my father what happened with Bobby one night at the dinner table. Sam tells him almost the same story.

"My God," my father yells, "my sons are such pussies that a blind kid beats them up! Go upstairs! No dessert for either of you!"

So Sam and I retreat, realizing that life just isn't fair.

A week or so later I become hell-bent on revenge. Not only am I a liar in the eyes of other students, and a nothing in my dad's, but now Bobby Kessler is telling everyone that I bullied him. Then he'd perform his fake cry.

Girls begin slapping me, calling me "a bully to the blind."

I realize I've had enough.

One day, after being hit once again with Bobby's braille machine during recess, I go to Dr. Perkins's office. I tell the principal that I hate Bobby, and I'll prove to him that he's the one who is the bully.

I have a plan.

For some reason Dr. Perkins goes along with it.

Why, I'll never know.

Maybe Dr. Perkins just wants to see me stumble, or maybe, deep down in his heart, he believes me.

But most likely, he is probably just plain bored.

And perhaps I'll amuse him.

I set things up so that Bobby and I are called to the principal's office at the same time.

When we arrive, Dr. Perkins is sitting behind his desk, as quiet as a mouse.

Even quieter.

"No one's here," I tell Bobby, "I suppose we should just sit down and wait."

"That cocksucker will be back soon," grunts Bobby, "but in the meantime, maybe I'll just kick your Jewboy ass!"

I glance over at Dr. Perkins and see a look of total shock on his face.

"Well," I say to the blind kid, "if you're gonna kick my ass, you gotta catch me first, Frankenstein!"

I then quickly run around the large desk and stand behind the principal.

"Over here," I yell at Bobby, as he extends both hands forward, grasping the air for my face. And my blood.

Bobby feels around some more and then finally grabs Dr. Perkins.

First he touches his tweed jacket and tie, then reaches up and feels his face. "Uh-oh," says Bobby.

And that was about the end of that.

BLOW HARD

SO THERE I AM, IN FRONT of my band instructor, Mr. Sigmond, with my trumpet in my hands. I'm in the tenth grade, and nervous as hell.

"Are you ready to play the piece?" asks Mr. Sigmond, for the third time and sort of annoyed.

"Um, almost," I say. "Just let me empty my spit-valve one more time."

I blow into my mouthpiece and just a tiny bit of drool comes out of the bottom tip of the trumpet. I look at Mr. Sigmond as my saliva slowly leaks onto the floor of the school's rehearsal room. He looks pissed, even with his funny little mustache and glaring bald spot.

"Are we ready, Mr. Tabb?" he demands.

"Yeah," I sigh, feeling my heart flutter.

"You've been fourth trumpet now for sometime," Mr. Sigmond explains, "and these auditions are being held for the entire school band to measure everyone's progress. I'm sure you'll do fine."

I look him in the eyes and know he is lying. He isn't doing this to place me as a first, second, third, or fourth trumpet. He wants to see if I can play trumpet.

At all.

And I'm about to show him.

                              *

I first decide to play trumpet in the fourth grade.

Well, I don't decide.

It's my father.

He decides he wants all his kids to play an instrument, so he can have the Tabb Family Band. He tells us that one day we can have a recital, and all our neighbors and friends can come and listen to us play. We'd be like the musical Brady Bunch.

Or the Partridge Family.

Or that Nazi family in that movie with Julie Andrews.

Whatever.

"George," my father asks me, "what instrument do you want to play?"

I tell him that I have no clue. He tells me I have to decide right there on the spot.

So I think about it for a few seconds.

"Flute," I finally say, because I know the case is tiny, easy to carry, and easy to lose. I also know only girls play them, and that would mean sitting next to them.

"Your sister already plays that," he replies, "and besides, you should play a man's instrument."

I try not to giggle.

"Um, piccolo," I say, because it's even smaller than the flute, easier to carry, and really easy to lose.

Plus, I know it will piss off my old man.

"Listen you little faggot," my father screams, "play a man's instrument!"

"Like yours?" I yell back at my father.

He slaps me in the face and says I should only open my mouth when he says I can.

Then he tells me about the tuba, trombone, and drums.

With my face stinging, I think about these instruments.

The tuba is way too fucking big, and there is no way in hell I'm going to carry that thing around.

And the drums were for dummies.

So I pick the trombone. I know it's rather large, and has a heavy case, but it is kind of cool. It slides up and down, in and out, and for some reason, that excites me. Also, you can sit behind someone and hit them in the head by extending the long thick brass.

"The trombone it is," says my dad.

The next day at school, I get stuck with the trumpet. It turns out too many other children had already picked trombone.

Oh well.

So I go to the local music store, and rent a trumpet. I look at the shiny instrument on display and it looks stupid.

But not too hard to learn. It only has very few buttons on it, compared to a flute, clarinet, oboe, or saxophone.

Easy, I think.

Three buttons, three notes.

How hard can it be?

I bring home the trumpet and show it to my dad. He says that the trumpet is not exactly what he wants for me, but it will do.

For now.

But he really wants me to learn piano, and learn to read music.

Whatever.

Then my father takes out a bugle he claims he got in the war, and starts to play "Taps."

It sounds horrible, like a horse farting.

Our two Great Danes run out of the room howling, along with our housekeepers poodle, Peachy.

We then hear Cybil from another room yelling that she can't hear the TV.

My dad, ignoring my stepmother, continues to play, and then plays something else I don't recognize. But it sounds an awful lot like "Deutschland Deutschland, Uber Alles."

*

My band instructor from the fourth to ninth grades is Mr. Berry.

And Mr. Berry rules. Big time.

During band rehearsals he manages to keep a bunch of spoiled-rotten brats entertained by telling funny jokes, and actually teaching some of the kids how to play their instruments.

But it's during separate instrument rehearsals, that he glows.

And he glows good, from the booze.

I'm a fourth trumpet and I like it that way.

No pressure. No expectations. No work. And no rehearsing.

Well, I did try to rehearse at home a few times.

Cybil purchases a "cone," which is sort of a mute for the instrument. So every once in a while I go to my room and blow into the damn thing for a few seconds, before stopping to read comic books. An hour later I go downstairs where Lester and Cybil approve of my practicing.

Idiots.

*

"Suicide is painless, and it comes in many stages," sings Mr. Berry at fourth trumpet rehearsals every week. It's the theme from *M.A.S.H.*

Only with the words.

Sometimes we would try and play along on our horns, but he'd wave us off and continue to sing.

Then he'd take huge swigs of whisky from a silver flask he always carried and moan in comfort, "Oh yeah."

Sometimes if we were lucky, he'd even let us have a sip or three.

Besides teaching us how to drink and sing songs about killing ourselves, Mr. Berry also made his best effort to teach us to read sheet music.

It seems everyone else understands it.

But not me.

I guess I'm musically dyslexic.

Sheet music looks like a Chinese menu to me.

So I just act like I can read it, and go along with everyone else.

Mr. Berry tries explaining clefs, timing, and rests to me, but I don't get that, either.

So Mr. Berry just tells me to play along, and fake it.

That he would watch out for me and lie to my father if necessary to help me avoid the beatings.

During our fourth trumpet rehearsals, all the kids play the songs and I don't.

I always complain that my braces hurt, or that I have the flu or something.

Mr. Berry always says it's quite all right and would sometimes offer me a swig. The other kids couldn't care less.

Sometimes as Mr. Berry directs us trumpets, I watch his hand go up and down and round and round, in a sort of drunken haze. He has this huge lump on his wrist the size of a golf-ball, and one day I ask him about it.

"That's my cyst," he tells me, reeking of alcohol. "My doctors say I'm gonna get gangrene, but I don't care."

"Cool," I say to Mr. Berry, wishing I could get gangrene too, whatever that is.

"Oh yeah Georgie baby," he says back to me, and then starts singing "Suicide is Painless" as usual.

What a guy.

*

As the years go by, Mr. Berry and I grow closer and closer. The guy kind of takes me under his wing, and tells me all sorts of neat adult stuff. About women and all.

In fact, he likes me so much, he sets up private rehearsals for me *only* and for a couple of years I rehearse alone with him. During class hours, of course.

Usually during math or gym.

Our rehearsals go great. I would walk in each week, and Mr. Berry would have already begun drinking. I would make like I was going to take out my trumpet, and he'd always tell me to put the damn thing away.

Then offer me a sip of whisky.

Then it was on to the facts of life.

Or, the facts of his life.

How he had sex a night earlier, or how his hand is in the process of falling off. How dying isn't so bad, and may actually be something to look forward to. Then it was more drinking and, finally, some horn playing. Sometimes it was the theme from *M.A.S.H.*, or sometimes it was Louie Armstrong. Whatever the guy would play sounded like gold.

Meanwhile, during full band rehearsals, Mr. Berry keeps an eye on me. And his flask.

While all the other kids play along to some John Phillips Sousa song or something, I just look at the music sheet and move my fingers. Making believe I'm playing. I don't make a sound, but certainly look like I do, with my cheeks bloated out and all. Mr. Berry had taught me well.

And he was right, no one noticed. It was great.

"You know, George," says Mr. Berry one day at our private rehearsal, "one day you are gonna get caught."

I look at him, puzzled.

"One day somebody is gonna find out you can't play," he continues, "then there'll be trouble."

I just look at him.

"But just remember George," explains Mr. Berry, with all seriousness, "suicide is painless."

Mr. Berry then takes a huge swig, yells "Oh yeah!" and gives me the rest of the flask.

When I finally make it to high school, I really miss the guy.

*

My first day at Greenwich High, we have band rehearsal.

Well, band auditions.

To see where we'll be placed in the school band.

Mr. Sigmond, our instructor, calls out my name and asks what trumpet I want to play.

"Fourth," I say, "of course."

He looks at me in shock, and asks why I want to be that *good* of a trumpet player.

Everyone laughs but me.

The irony gets lost somewhere in my tenth grade mind, so I just shrug my shoulders.

"You've been fourth trumpet for sometime," Mr. Sigmond says, "I can see it from your records."

More laughs.

I'm afraid of what's coming next.

"Let's hear you play," says Mr. Sigmond.

I feel my heart drop into my left foot.

I look at the sheet music and know that the shit is about to hit the fan. This day had been coming for years; I'd just been putting it off.

"Tell you what," says the band instructor, "we'll do this in private. After school."

So I get a two-hour reprieve.

*

Alone with Mr. Sigmond, I knew I couldn't fake it. So when he asks me for the third time to play, I prepare to blow into the trumpet, but first I empty my spit-valve again.

"Okay," growls the band instructor, holding up his directing stick, "a *one*, and a *two*, and a *three* and a—"

And that's when I put my trumpet down on my lap.

"You can't play, can you?," asks Mr. Sigmond.

"Nope," I say, as I stare at my reflection in the trumpet on my lap, filled with shame.

"I figured as much," says Mr. Sigmond, "during rehearsal earlier, I saw that you weren't playing. You can't even fake it well."

I say nothing, but feel rage swell up inside of me. If there is one thing I'm good at in my whole miserable life it's faking it.

But this putz is telling me I'm not even good at that?

"Look, George," Mr. Sigmond explains with a slight smile, "the truth of the matter is we need all the instruments in this band we can get. As you know, we're a marching band as well as a recital band."

I nod my head in agreement.

"Just fake it a while longer," he explains, "and I'll let you slide this year. But next year you're out."

I nod my head again.

"We'll need you this year," he continues, "because we are competing in the marching nationals held in Toronto. What do ya think?"

I think I'm about to vomit, then quit, but quickly remember my father, and the ass-whipping he'll give me if he ever finds out what I've been doing, or *not* doing, all these years.

"It's a deal," I say to Mr. Sigmond.

We shake hands.

That year, I become the school's first fifth trumpet, and eventually do make it to Canada, where we take first or second place.

But after that, I never touch the trumpet again.

I learn to fake guitar.

A Turtle's Tale

"GEORGE," MY FATHER YELLS FROM our driveway, "get your lazy thirteen-year-old ass out here right now!"

From my bedroom, I debate ignoring my father and finishing the Spiderman comic book I'm so engrossed in. I'm up to a part where Doc Ock escapes from prison again, kidnaps Aunt May and Spidey is torn between saving his aunt, and getting some action from his hot girlfriend.

"George, you little fuck," yells my dad, "get out here now. Don't make me come up there!"

"Don't make me come up there" is slang for kicking my ass. I'm out on the driveway in about five seconds.

"Look at that," says my dad, pointing at two white kittens on the driveway. One is lying on its side, eyes closed and mouth open. The other has its tail in the air and head against the black, tar pavement.

There's blood next to each.

"What happened to those kitties?" I ask my dad.

"You tell me," he says, "and it's kitty."

I look closely at the kittens, and see that my dad is right. It's one cat, split in half at the midsection. The tail end has no head. The head end has no tail. I almost puke.

"Well?" asks my dad.

I tell him I don't know what happened. But I did understand why he was asking me.

My brothers and I used to take cats, kittens, and other small creatures, and make "roller-coasters" for them. We'd put them in cardboard boxes, then find some unused wallpaper and slide the animals in the boxes down "the track" from the back porch.

Sometimes the cats would fall out. But we didn't worry, they'd always land on their feet. We never *really* hurt any cats, just gave them fun rides.

Besides, catracide wasn't our style.

As my dad and I stare at the white fluffs of bloody fur on the driveway, suddenly the kitten's eyes open, as does its mouth. Blood then pours out, over its pink tongue.

I go over to the grass and puke my brains out.

When I finish, I look back at my dad, and he mouths the word "pussy" at me.

Then, our housekeeper, Attie, comes strolling out of the house. My dad takes Attie by the arm, and shows her the dead kitten.

"Damn if I ain't seen that before," says Attie.

Then she goes on to explain that when she lived in Alabama, she saw lots of dead animals that looked like that. She explained that the dead cat was the result of an overly large, and overly hungry, snapping turtle.

"Snapping turtle?" I ask Attie.

I'd seen them in our pond in the woods, but they didn't look big enough to bite off my nose. Or even my small toe.

"It's a goddamn snapping turtle," swears Attie, "and you boys best find it before it eats your dogs, or some of you chilren."

She always calls us "chilren."

Then Attie leaves my dad and I alone with the dead kitten.

"What are you looking at," screams my dad at me. "Go inside

the garage, get a fucking shovel, and clean up this fucking mess."

*

About a week later, while my brothers and I are riding down rocky dirt-covered hills in old steel barrels, cutting ourselves against the rusted metal, we stumble upon one of our baby goats at the bottom of the hill.

It's missing its stomach.

"What the fuck happened to the goat?" asks my brother, Sam.

I hit him, hard.

"Don't you fucking swear, Sam," I say.

"That's fuckin' sick," exclaims Luke, my other brother.

I hit him as well.

That night, when my dad returns home from work, I lead him and Attie to where the dead goat is busy attracting flies and maggots.

"P-U," says Attie, "that goat smells worse than Luke's farts!"

"Do you think it's the turtle?" asks my dad, knowing nothing about nature except that it's meant to be torn down and paved over.

Attie tells us it is, and even shows us the bite marks around the belly of the bloody beast. Of course I walk about five feet away and throw up.

This time, though, my dad doesn't call me a pussy.

He just says calmly, "Go in the fucking garage, get a fucking shovel, and clean up this fucking mess you useless fuck."

*

A couple of days later, my next door neighbor, Andy, calls me and tells me to come over and listen to the new Kiss album with him while we go fishing. I'm busy trying to figure out how to play with myself, so I tell him let's do it some other time.

"I got a case of Coors," he says.

Five minutes later, I'm down the street.

"I just got the new Kiss album," explains Andy, who gives me all his Izod shirts when he grows out of them, "we can blast the stereo out the window and go bass fishing!"

I look around at Andy's house and his large pond in his backyard.

It seems like a fine idea to me.

"Where's the beer?" I ask him.

Two minutes later, Andy exits his house with Kiss blaring on the stereo, two fishing rods in one hand and a case of Coors in the other.

Cool.

We each find good rocks to sit on, and cast our rods into the pond. As "Calling Dr. Love" blasts from his stereo, Andy asks me if we've had any dead animal problems lately.

I crack open a Coors, banned this side of the Mississippi, and tell him we have.

I explain to him about the loss of the kitten and the goat, and how I buried them and stuck crosses made of sticks over their graves.

"But you're a Jew," says Andy, "why not a Star Of David?"

I just stare at him.

He's a fellow Jew amongst the gentiles.

Andy then explains that he also found a kitten on his driveway, or rather, half a kitten, and a couple of dead ducks in the grass.

I tell him I him I didn't know he even owned a cat. Or any pets.

"It was one of yours," he replies.

"Oh," I reply.

It figures. We had over thirty-eight cats, give or take a couple.

Take, I guess.

Andy pops open a Coors and guzzles it.

*

About an hour later, as we both finish our fourth beer, we see a strange sight.

A mother duck, with all her ducklings swimming behind her, quacks loudly as the last in line of her babies suddenly vanishes beneath the water.

"Whoa," I say, "Jaws."

We keep watching, as another duckling disappears. Then blood rises to the surface.

"Holy fucking motherfucker shit!" exclaims Andy.

I hit him.

He's not supposed to swear.

Suddenly, I feel a nibble on my fishing line and snap the reel back. I land a pretty-huge big-mouthed bass and try to free the hook from the fish's eye.

"Leave it on the line," explains Andy, "I have an idea."

Andy then instructs me to cast the fish out into the water, near where we saw the last duckling go down, and reel it in slowly.

I do as I am told. After all, Andy is a full year older than me. And he's holding the beer.

I throw the bass out into the water, and start to reel it in slowly. It fights like crazy, but with a hook through its eye it isn't likely to go anywhere.

As I reel it in closer and closer, I see a huge shadow following behind it.

So does Andy.

"Holy motherfucking cat crap," exclaims Andy, "do you fucking see what I see?"

I hit him, then tell him I do.

Behind the fish, paddling very slowly, is a *huge*, I mean *gigantic,* turtle.

"It's fucking Gamera!" I yell, unable to contain myself.

Andy just nods his head, sips his Coors through a straw, and lets out a low whistle. We both stare at the monster that could probably kill Godzilla. It's at least two feet long, without the tail, with a head like a tree stump.

"Whatta we do?" I ask Andy, with more than a quiver in my voice. I'm fucking scared. The turtle could bite off our penises, which wouldn't be fair since I hadn't even figured out how to work mine.

"Just reel it in slowly," explains Andy, "I'm gonna run in the garage and get a metal tub. When it comes out of the water, we'll catch it!"

Sounds good to me.

But I still back up about ten feet from the water.

I reel the bass onto the shore of the pond. The fish, now flopping around on the muddy ground, is followed by Gamera, who exits the water slowly.

Andy returns rather quickly with a round metal basin and then throws it over the huge-ass turtle. Its tail sticks out, but we have the beast under the tub.

"We got the motherfucking cocksucking son-of-a-bitch asshole turtle!" Andy yells.

I high-five him.

We listen as the turtle bonks its head against the side of the tub, trying to escape. This goes on for a couple of minutes, as we just stand there, drinking our fifth and sixth Coors.

"What do we do now?" I finally ask Andy, as he stands atop the tub, so it stops moving.

"George," says Andy, in all seriousness, "it is our mission to destroy this turtle."

"Destroy?" I ask, somewhat confused.

"Kill," explains Andy, "this monster has taken the lives of many animals, some we may have loved. Our job as a society is to be judge, jury, and executioner. We must carry out its death sentence and slay the beast."

I suddenly find myself jealous of Andy. It seems he's learning some cool stuff over at Brunswick, an all boys private school my father refuses to let us attend.

"Um, how are we gonna do that?" I ask, snapping myself out of my own thoughts.

"With this," exclaims Andy.

He quickly runs into his garage, and grabs one of the largest axes I've ever seen.

"We're gonna cut the fucker's head off," he exclaims.

We both grab large sticks and try to flip the tub over. Once we have, the turtle raises its ugly, tree-stump head in the air toward us and snaps.

Phantom pain shoots through my groin.

Andy slowly circles the animal and, as he does, it follows him with its eyes.

"Andy," I scream, "if you're gonna chop off its head, you've gotta get closer!"

"Shut up Tabb, you pussy," yells Andy. "You wanna try?"

I think about how the turtle ate the kitten. I think about how the turtle ate the goat.

Then I think about my dad making me dig holes to bury dead bodies.

And how I *hate* yard work.

"Yeah," I say to Andy, "gimme the ax."

Andy hands me the heavy tool. It feels nice in my hands. It's new and has a nice, shiny blade.

Good for killing.

Just like the one in *Night of the Living Dead*.

As Andy diverts the turtle's attention with a long stick, I sneak up behind it and whack it in its nubby head with the sharp blade. The impact is so hard it feels like my wrists break.

Then, nothing.

The turtle, still interested in Andy's stick, seems not to have felt a thing. So I whack it again and again.

It feels like I'm hammering a rock.

"Lemme try," exclaims Andy, as he takes away the ax and gives me his stick.

I start to poke the turtle as Andy begins to chop away at its head.

Finally he draws some blood. After about thirty whacks.

"I got the fucker," exclaims Andy.

We both watch as blood begins to pour out of a deep slice in the turtle's neck. But it doesn't seem to phase the damn thing. It just keeps snapping at our stick, and trying to stare us down.

"I know how to fuck him up," yells Andy as he runs into his house, "I'll be right back."

*

Andy returns a few minutes later, after turning over the Kiss record and grabbing a can of salt.

"Salt?" I ask him, as I keep the turtle at bay by poking its slashed neck with the stick.

"Yeah, it'll make it go nuts and die," answers Andy.

Like I said, they learn all the cool stuff at Brunswick.

Andy goes over to the turtle and pours the whole can on its

neck. Now the turtle's head is red and white.

Still, nothing.

Then, suddenly, it starts snapping at the air like crazy.

"See," says Andy, "it's in pain, the salt is killing it."

The turtle continues to snap at the air, and lets out some really disturbing noises. I almost feel sorry for it, but then remember the holes I had to dig.

We stand there watching the turtle snap at the air as one Kiss song ends and another begins.

Suddenly, as if taking its cue from the stereo, the turtle rushes at Andy and me. It had been about fifteen feet away, but in about one second, was five.

We scream like babies and run away as fast as we can. The turtle follows us, leaving a trail of blood behind it.

"Holy motherfucking shit!" yells Andy as we run across his yard.

I just scream nonsense and start to cry.

Gamera is going to kill me.

"Tabb," yells Andy, as the monster chases us around his lawn, "distract it and I'll catch it!"

Distract it?

Fuck that shit. I'm getting the hell away from that thing before it turns me into a girl. As I haul ass for the driveway, I turn around and see Andy following the turtle who is following me. In his hands is the metal tub.

Finally Andy throws the tub over it and, once again, it's captured.

We both let out audible sighs, and then Andy points at my tears and calls me a sissy.

I point at his and tell him he's one, too.

We open more beer and sit on the tub with the turtle knocking underneath. We couldn't kill the damn thing.

"Why don't we drop a nuclear bomb on it?" I ask Andy.

"We don't have one, George," is his reply.

"Oh yeah," I say, "how about we blast it with a phaser?"

"Shut the fuck up, you watch too much television," he answers.

So we just sit there on the tub, with the turtle making funny noises, and bonking its head against the sides.

"Nuclear bomb, huh?" says Andy, scratching his chin.

"I got it," he suddenly screams, "M-80s—we'll blow up the son-of-a-bitch."

Andy tells me to hold down the fort, and the turtle, and he'll run in and get a few.

Fucking Brunswick. They always get all the good stuff.

As Andy runs into the house, I stand on the basin. No way was I going to sit on it alone.

Andy returns with a fist full of M-80s. He lights one and throws it under the tub. We get away, fast.

"Bonk!" is the sound we hear.

We lift away the tub with a long stick and see the turtle, smoke surrounding it, still snapping at the air.

"I don't think that worked," I tell Andy.

He tells me to shut-up, that he has an idea. He walks close to the turtle, lights an M-80, throws it near its head, and then runs back to me.

What I see next is totally amazing.

Apparently, the wounded turtle, with its slashed neck, in a salt covered frenzy, mistakes the M-80 for something to eat, and snatches it up with its jaws.

We watch as the turtle tries to swallow the quarter stick of dynamite. Then we hear a loud *pop*, and see lots of smoke. When it clears, the turtle looks just fine, except for its bottom jaw that's hanging to the left by a thin piece of tissue.

The turtle sees us and starts snapping at the air in our direction. Only now, its bottom jaw just flops around sadly.

"It lives," I say to Andy.

He nods.

We watch as it tries to bite the air, then the tissue holding its jaw finally tears. I feel myself start to get sick.

"Andy, we gotta kill the damn thing, put it out of its misery," I explain, "it's the right thing to do."

"You are such a pussy, Tabb," is his reply.

But he knew I was right. Even though the beast had killed two cats, a goat, and at least two ducks, it didn't deserve to be tortured by a couple of kids like us. It was a creature of habit.

Andy runs back inside his house again and this time returns with a rifle.

"What the fuck?" I manage to mumble.

"My dad hides it in his closet," Andy explains, "and I found some ammo in his locked drawer."

Andy shows me a fist full of .22-caliber bullets and lets me hold the gun.

"Awesome," I say, but then ask, "why didn't we just use this in the first place?"

"If my dad finds out I know where his gun is, and how to use it," explains the fourteen-year-old, as he pops open another beer, "he'll kill me. Let's just waste the turtle, and put the gun back as fast as we can. My dad will be home in twenty minutes."

"Neato," I say.

Andy then opens the rifle, and loads a bullet into the chamber. He stands about six feet away and shoots at the turtle. The bullet hits the turtle's shell, and the animal starts to spin in circles.

"Cool," we both say in unison.

"My turn," I say to Andy and we struggle over the gun, spilling our beers.

"Do you even know how to use it?" he asks.

I tell him I do. That I've seen lots of them used on TV.

So Andy hands me the gun.

I load the gun and aim it at the turtle's head. I gently squeeze the trigger and fire. Dirt flies up next to the turtle's head.

"Ha-ha, you missed," yells Andy. "My turn!"

He grabs the gun, loads it, and shoots the turtle right in the face. Its lower jaw explodes into a cloud of bone and blood.

We both look at the animal.

And it looks at us.

Alive.

With no lower jaw. But it keeps bobbing its head up and down, like it is trying to bite.

"Gimme the gun," I say to Andy, grabbing the rifle and spilling more beer.

I load it and tell Andy I'm gonna put an end to this once and for all. Andy says he'll enjoy watching me try.

I walk up to the turtle, stick the barrel of the rifle down whatever was left of its throat, and pull the trigger.

Turtle guts fly everywhere, especially on to Andy's father's gun.

"Now look what ya fuckin' did," exclaims Andy, "how the fuck am I gonna clean this before my dad gets home?"

We both look at the gun, covered in blood, and the headless turtle on the ground. It's tail moves for a few seconds, then finally stops. We both look at one another and then hi-five.

We slayed the beast.

We spend the next fifteen minutes cleaning Andy's dad's gun as best as we can. We use toilet cleaner we find in the bathroom and it seems to work just fine.

The gun is all shiny and clean when Andy puts it back in his dad's closet.

Back outside again, we stare at the turtle.

Suddenly, Andy's dad pulls into the driveway in his new Porsche and parks. He's wearing a nice gray business suit, and his hair is slicked back like everyone else who takes the 7:05 to Grand Central Station.

"Whatcha boys doin?" he asks as he walks into the backyard where we're standing over the dead turtle.

"We killed a snapping turtle with an ax," Andy yells out, before I can say anything, "It's the one that was eating the ducks and cats."

Andy's dad stares at the headless turtle.

"Where's it's head?" he asks.

Andy tells him we threw it in the pond.

Andy's dad then looks at the basin and the bloody ax on the ground.

"Well," he says, "it looks to me like you boys did a mighty fine job. But it must have been hard to kill it with just an ax."

We shrug our shoulders.

"You should have used my rifle," Andy's father explains.

We nod our heads and say nothing.

Suddenly I can't help but burp.

The stench of Coors fills the air.

"You boys been drinking my beer, again?" asks Andy's dad.

We both nod our heads. There's no use in lying about that.

"Well," he smiles, "it's okay. I guess I'm glad you *didn't* use the rifle."

Andy and I have stupid grins on our faces.

"Now," he starts, "why don't you boys get some shovels and bury that damn thing before it stinks up the yard."

We both nod our heads, but after Andy's dad goes inside, I bolt. The fuck if I'm going to bury that turtle.

*

Andy remains mad at me for about three weeks, but eventually calls me about a bottle of Jack Daniel's and a Peter Frampton album.

A Dog's Wife

Bear.

Even his name still sends chills up my spine.

But he wasn't really a bear.

Not technically, anyway.

He was more of a, well, big fucking dog.

Huge.

On his hind legs he stood well over six-and-a-half feet tall.

With lots of black fur, he outweighed me by at least a hundred pounds, even by the time I got to eighth grade.

When *it* happened.

*

I had just turned fourteen.

After an exhausting day at Central Junior High in Greenwich, Connecticut.

The bus ride home that day was no different than most other days. Name calling, fists flying, and now, cigarette-smoking.

In the back of the bus, of course.

Anyway, the main name-callers are the usual bullies. And kids who used their fists had yet to meet my lunch box. But added to these brats were now Luke's little friends, Michael Ludwig and

Norman Freeman. Both of whom exit at our bus stop.

As we step off the bus, Luke apologizes for not helping me fight off the Gangs Of Greenwich that day. I think he was too busy getting stoned and staring at pictures in porno magazines with his pals in the back of the bus. With weed and naked nookie, they no doubt secured from our new/old bus driver, Jackie the hippie.

Who still smelled the same.

Awful.

"It's okay, Luke," I tell my brother.

And it is.

The kid isn't expected to fight *everyday*.

Just every other.

"You're such a kike," says Michael Ludwig, shaking me from my thoughts on our long way home that day.

Puzzled, I ask him if he means "kite."

I'd heard the word before and couldn't understand what I had to do with long rolls of string and oversized flying plastic bats or boxes.

"Kike," replies Michael, "I said kike!"

Pressing him as to what it means, he confesses that his dad told him my whole family were "kikes," the plural of "kike," but he actually wasn't sure of the meaning. He knew it involved my father not going to 'Nam.

When I ask what *'Nam* is, he tells me it is where Jim Hutton was killed and John Wayne earned his Special Forces badge.

When I ask him what the fuck he's talking about, he mumbles something about the "Battle of the Green Berets," then punches me in the mouth.

Hard.

Then Norman Freeman begins to laugh hysterically. Out of control.

"What's so funny?" Luke asks his friend.

"Your brother is *so gay*," he replies.

"Shut up, Norman," I say to the creep who lives on Londenderry Drive, but for some reason is following us home.

"Make me," is his smart seventh-grade reply.

So, of course, I try.

I attack him, swinging wildly at his face and head. I land a few good punches before Michael Ludwig and Luke break it up.

"If you guys wanna really fight, you should do it in front of my house," explains Ludwig.

"Why?" I demand, as Luke holds me back from kicking Norman Freeman's pussy ass. I'd done it before with a snow shovel, why not do it again with my fists?

"Because I have boxing gloves," replies Michael Ludwig, "and it could be a real fight, like to the death!"

For some reason, this makes lots of sense to our seventh and eighth grade minds.

Of course, the idea of aiming one of Mr. Luder's semi-automatic weapons at Norman had also crossed my mind. Or one of his pistols, rifles, or even hunting knives.

As we walk up Guinea Road towards our house, Norman keeps telling me he's gonna kick my ass and that I'm a pussy.

This coming from a guy whose brown hair stands straight up on the back of his head like a stick.

"Fuck you, Alfalfa," I say to the little fuck.

As we approach my driveway I puss out. I explain that violence never settles anything, that fighting is bad and if Norman has a problem with me, we should try to discuss it.

Norman and Michael's answer is to grab my arms and legs, and actually carry me a few hundred feet to the Ludwig's driveway.

While I'm being taken hostage, I look to Luke for help.

He just looks back at me, with fear in his eyes.

I feel sorry for him.

Finally, I'm dropped.

Head first.

"Ready to die, Tabb?" asks Norman as he puts up his fists in a fighter's stance.

"Wait," yells Michael Ludwig, "I gotta run inside and get the boxing gloves from my sisters. It won't work without them!"

I take a stance like Norman, and we don't take our eyes off one another for even a second.

Luke just watches, helpless.

"Kick his ass, George," Luke says to me.

I wink at him. Like I see heroes do in movies.

Finally Michael returns from his house with red boxing gloves.

And something else.

His dog.

Bear.

And he looks scary.

*

Norman and I put on the boxing gloves as Michael, Luke, and Bear stand by and watch.

Bear is drooling, of course.

After Michael and Luke finish tying up the strings on our gloves, the fight begins with Michael yelling, "Ding-ding!"

I come out from my side of the driveway swinging, and land a few great punches in Freeman's freckled face. Norman then nails me in the breadbasket a few times, but it doesn't hurt. We continue swinging until I luckily hit Norman so hard in the head he falls to his knees.

"Had enough?" I ask as he kneels there, blood pouring from

his nose and mouth, with a stunned look on his face.

He says nothing, so I guess he has.

I turn around and ask Luke to please untie my gloves, telling him it is over.

As Luke complies, Norman gets up behind me, finds a stick the size of a two-by-four and, with his boxing gloves still on, hits me in the side of the head with it.

*

The next thing I know, everyone is upside down, staring at me.

Then I feel grass itching the sides of my face and dirt support-ing the back of my head.

I must have landed in the yard.

I try to get up, but feeling dizzy, flop back down.

Norman laughs his evil little laugh, while Luke and Michael just stare at me in disbelief.

"Ha-ha, Tabb, you kite," screams Norman. "I got you, fag!"

"Kike," I manage to spit out.

"Whatever," says Norman, blood still pouring from his nose. Then he kicks me in the side.

Hard.

Suddenly Bear, who was sitting, drooling, and watching the whole event, gets up on all fours and starts running toward Norman. Norman screams like the little girl he is and hauls ass. Bear chases him around a few trees, furiously barking. He's so loud it feels like my eardrums are going to explode.

Norman quickly climbs up a tree and screams helplessly to be rescued.

Michael laughs, Luke says nothing.

I find myself smiling as I watch Bear paw at the tree with the little monkey in it.

Eventually, when I'm able to speak clearly, I say "good boy!"

Big mistake.

The dog looks at me, at my eyes.

Then he runs over while I'm still on the ground, dizzy and unable to stand.

"Tabb," sneers Ludwig, "you should have shut your trap. Now he likes you. And you *don't* want him liking you!"

I'm about to ask Michael what he's talking about, when suddenly Bear climbs on top of me and stands on my stomach and chest.

"Get him offa me," I manage to eke out, barely able to breathe.

"Too late," replies Ludwig, "I can't."

"Can't?" asks Luke, "or won't?"

"You'll just have to wait until he's through," explains Michael Ludwig, laughing so hard he's clutching his stomach.

Michael just laughs a lot more.

As does Norman, still hiding up in the tree.

Suddenly Bear starts to do what our housekeeper's poodle does to our legs.

Only Bear's well over two hundred pounds.

And instead of a tiny pink eraser-tip penis, he's got the whole damn pencil.

Actually, more like a Louisville Slugger.

*

Bear positions his legs at my sides, ensuring my body stays in place.

He then begins to grind away at my crotch, with his monster wiener.

As he violently thrusts and thrusts, he puts his mouth near my left ear and growls, letting me know that if I try anything, he'll rip my face off.

Soon I begin to cry.

His dog dick is really sharp and is tearing apart my shirt.

Plus, every once in a while, he nips my ear just to let me know who's boss.

"Cry-baby, cry-baby," yells Norman who, by now, has climbed down from his perch.

"Tabb," laughs Ludwig, "looks like you like it ruff! R-U-F-F!"

Meanwhile, Bear continues to hump me. Somehow, I manage to turn over to my stomach, so Bear starts to do me on my ass. At times, he places his entire weight on my back, making it impossible to move or breathe.

The tears pour down my face.

"Help me," I cry to my brother and his loser friends. "Please."

Luke looks at me again, helplessly, while Norman and Michael laugh so hard they're hugging each other.

Bear suddenly begins to thrust faster and harder.

He then grabs my curly, brown afro with his teeth and lets out the meanest growl I've ever heard.

"It's almost over, Tabb," Ludwig says.

"How would you know?" I sob.

"He did it to me last week," Michael Ludwig replies, smiling.

Suddenly Bear's body goes into a giant doggie-spasm.

I then feel my back and butt get flooded with a warm liquid.

"Ewwww!" squeals Norman, in delight.

*

Finally, Bear steps off of me, licks my face with his sandpaper tongue, and runs back into the Ludwig home.

Crying, I stand up and curse my brother and his lousy friends.

Norman and Michael laugh so hard they choke, while all Luke can manage is a weak smile.

"Your fucking dog pissed on me," I scream at Ludwig.

"Um, I wouldn't say *pissed*," says Ludwig.

Then he and Norman laugh some more and I slowly make my way home.

*

A couple of years later I heard Bear was involved in a car accident. Ten thousand dollars worth of damage was done to a Rolls Royce. The dog, of course, was fine.

STIFF COMPETITION

SO, THERE I AM, NOT only in front of many of my classmates and their parents, but also in front of what seems to be the entire population of Stamford, Connecticut.

I stand there, with my dopey-looking headgear on, and shorts that I hate to wear. I'm also wearing a Greenwich High School T-shirt and Tiger brand wrestling shoes.

I feel ready to faint. I don't want to be here, I want to be home, launching frogs in Estes Rockets; riding up and down my driveway on my cool ass Chopper bike; looking at the *Hustler* magazines I have hidden out in the woods behind a rock in a stone fence, next to a six-pack of Coors.

I look at my opponent, Brandon, a name I'll never forget, and it looks like he doesn't want to be here, either. He'd rather be home playing with frogs or riding up and down his driveway as well. Or even reading porno, although he looks like the type that would never admit it; his clothes are way too clean, and his hair way too straight. He's definitely a *Sports Illustrated* swimsuit edition kind of guy.

"You guys ready to mix it up?" asks the referee to both of us, as he stands there in his black-and-white-striped shirt, whistle between his lips.

"Um, errr," I mumble.

"Well?" demands the referee.

"Go Tabb, go!" yells Coach Mathers from the side of the mat.

Suddenly my whole school starts to cheer, as does Stamford. The noise is deafening and I feel like I'm gonna puke.

"Okay," says the referee, "ready, set . . . "

I look Brandon in the eyes; he looks me in the shoes. He's more afraid then I am. Then the whistle blows and it begins.

*

I never intended to be on the wrestling team.

Ever.

It was all my father's big idea, like being in the school band.

"George," he says to me one day, "when I was your age I played football for my school."

I just look at him.

"Go out for football," he explains, "it might even give you a chance to go on a date. But I doubt it."

I tell my dad that I'm in ninth grade, I weigh ninety-six pounds, and will be pulverized.

"But it will make you a man," he says.

Then my stepmother, Cybil, who is lurking behind us, decides to chime in.

"Your father's right," she says, "guys who play with the pig skin always get the girls."

I just look at her.

"Besides," she continues, "they're always so well hung. Especially the black ones."

My father tells Cybil to leave the room.

"Look son," he says when she's gone; his use of the word *son*, in that tone, that means business. "If you don't go out for football, you may as well just pack your bags and go live on a park bench in the junkie-filled streets of New York City."

I ask him if I can go out for baseball, instead.

"Oh, okay," he moans, then calls me a pussy.

So, in ninth grade, I try out for the baseball team and don't even make first cut because the one-armed kid in my grade can throw, catch, pitch, and hit better then I ever could.

So, instead, I go out for wrestling.

I do ask a coach about football, but he tells me to come back when I hit puberty.

Coach Williams is the guy in charge of wrestling, and I like him. He has a big Jewish afro like me, and looks like Gabe Kaplin from *Welcome Back, Kotter*.

"So you want to be a wrestler?" asks Coach Williams, the first day of practice.

"No," I reply, "I want to be a filmmaker, but my dad wants me to be on a sports team."

"Oh," replies Coach Williams, then explains to me that there are no tryouts and everyone makes the team; like some sort of communist sport.

"Actually, " I tell the coach, "You can just keep me on the bench the whole season if you want, I won't mind."

He laughs. Then he tells me to go change into my shorts.

*

The first day of practice is so tough that I walk around for an entire week sore as hell. My neck is so stiff I can't turn sideways and it feels like my groin is on fire. It sucks.

During our first week we learn to do spins, which is when one guy puts his chest on the other guy's back and then goes around in circles. Once every revolution your dick is in some guy's face, or your face in some guy's dick.

We also learn to start wrestling from the kneeling position. This time, your face is up some guy's ass, or vice versa.

Then there's the kneeling takedown, where you reach between some guy's legs and grab his arms, knocking him down fast. Of course, your hand and arm rub up against his penis, which feels rather odd. Soon I begin to feel uncomfortable with the whole wrestling thing.

"George," says Coach Williams to me around the second or third week of practice, "you don't seem to be really going tough, what's the problem?"

I hate that term.

"Going tough."

It's what all the other kids and coaches say.

"Go Tough!" Whatever the hell that means.

"No problem-o, Coach Williams," I tell the man and his afro.

"You're not getting into it, what's wrong?" he asks.

I explain to the coach that, although this seems neat and cool, I don't really feel comfortable grabbing other guys' crotches, or sticking my head up their asses.

"Are you afraid wrestling will turn you gay?" he asks, with a very serious look on his face.

"I don't know what I'm afraid of," I reply.

*

The first match of the Central Junior High team is against Darien.

The second, Stamford.

The third, Ridgefield, and fourth, New Canaan.

I sit on the bench at every match and am very happy about that.

I get to watch other guys pound each other into the mats, win or lose, and I don't get a scratch.

Then comes the fifth match, against Norwalk.

It's a home match, meaning at our school, and lots of people turn out, including my brothers and sisters.

"Ya ready to wrestle today, Tabb?" asks Coach Williams.

"Naw," I reply, "but I'm more than happy to watch as usual."

"Go into the locker room," yells Coach Williams, "and saddle up! You're wrestling first today."

I ask him why I have to wrestle, *especially* first.

"Because you're the smallest guy in the smallest weight class," is his reply.

I go to the locker room and suit up.

As I put on my wrestling uniform, I realize I hate it. The shoes are for sissies, and the shorts are too short and tight.

I'm also not liking the v-neck shirt either, which shows everyone that I have no chest hair. I may as well just announce that I haven't reached puberty yet.

I return to a very crowded gymnasium, with lots of people cheering. I hold my arms up in the air like I see boxers do, just for the hell of it.

"Ready Tabb?" asks Coach Williams as I feel a cool breeze blow across my tights.

"I guess so," I reply.

The score board lights up and my name is on it, in huge letters. It makes me smile.

Also on the board is the kid's name from Norwalk. It's Taylor, and he looks rather large, especially for our weight class.

The referee blows the whistle and the Taylor kid comes at me. Fast.

The next thing I know, I'm face down on the mat, and he's trying to turn me over for a pin.

I refuse to move, and it seems like he's trying to flip me over for hours.

"Just give up, you pussy," the Taylor kid whispers to me as he drives his knee into my side.

"Just roll over," he continues, "and let me pin you."

But I won't move. I don't want my first match to end like this. Plus, I'm really starting to hate this guy.

Taylor drives his chin into my shoulders and bends my arm backwards, trying to make me turn over from pain.

He also, for some reason, drives his crotch into my rear end.

"Roll over, faggot, and make it easy on yourself," he whispers in my ear as his chin digs deeper into my back. I feel pain shoot down my legs.

Then something odd happens. During all this body contact, I start to get an erection.

"Thirty more seconds of pain, motherfucker," snarls Taylor. "Turn the fuck over, faggot."

"Fuck off," I manage to hiss as tears of pain run down my cheeks.

There is no way he, or anyone else, is going to see that I popped a boner.

Then the whistle blows.

"Okay guys," says the referee, "break it up."

Taylor gets off of me and stands up. I stay on the mat, face down.

"You can get up now," the ref tells me.

"Do I really have to?" I ask.

"Get up you fuckin' pussy," yells Taylor, as his coach grabs him by the neck and drags him away.

"No," I scream back at Taylor.

"Are you hurt?" asks the referee with a confused look on his face.

I think about it. If I say I am, then perhaps I'll get a stretcher and no one will see my enlarged penis.

But I realize they'll turn me over, anyway.

"No," I tell the referee, "I'll get up."

And I do so, very slowly.

As I hold my hands in front of my wang, I try to think about dead babies.

I try to think about dog shit.

I try to think about throwing rocks at small animals in the woods.

But, instead, I think about the porno magazine hidden there, with all those breasts and vaginas.

My erection grows stronger.

I limp over to my side of the mat as Coach Williams approaches me.

"What's wrong George?" he asks. "Why are your hands over your crotch? Did he knee you?"

"Umm," I stammer.

"That's illegal," my coach continues, "we can have the referee recall the match."

"Errrr," I continue stammering.

"What's wrong George?" demands the coach.

"I sorta popped a boner," I whisper in his ear.

Coach Williams starts to laugh.

Not loud.

But loud enough.

"What's so funny Coach Williams?" asks Joe Easton, the captain of our team.

"Nothing," replies Coach Williams, trying to keep a

straight face.

I look at my coach, and feel more tears beginning to well up.

"Look George," explains Coach Williams, "it's perfectly normal for boys your age to get erections at strange times."

I sort of nod my head.

"Don't worry about it," the coach continues, "just stand up and go on about your business, wrestling."

With that, he pats me on the shoulder and sends me back in front of the entire school.

My hands block my crotch, of course. I hear lots of whispering from the stands.

"Are you ready, boys?" asks the referee again.

We both nod our heads.

Then the referee's eyes, as well as Taylor's, go to my hands.

"Is there a problem?" asks the ref.

"No problem at all, sir," is my response.

The whistle blows and the next thing I know I'm on the ground again, with Taylor on top of me.

"Turn over now, Jew boy," snarls Taylor, "and it'll all be over."

I'm about to tell him to fuck-off when he bends my arm so hard I yelp and roll over.

"Three, two, one," counts the referee. "You're pinned!"

Taylor continues to lay on top of me and I'm quite sure he feels my erection against his stomach.

"You guys can get up now," says the referee.

"Ha," says Taylor, slowly getting to his feet, "you really are a faggot."

*

After the match with Norwalk, I'm lucky enough to warm the

bench the rest of my ninth grade wrestling career. Coach Williams never said anything about that event, but he always smiled at me a bit funnily after that day.

I'm elated when I start tenth grade at a different school.

*

My new coach, Coach Mathers, is some sort of doctor. I don't know what kind, but outside of wrestling practice everyone calls him *Dr.* Mathers. He has a beard, short brown hair, and looks very smart.

"George," Coach Mathers says to me the first day of tryouts, "I'm not even putting you through an audition for varsity, you're the lightest guy to go out for the team."

Uh-oh.

"You're automatically going to be on the team, isn't that great?" exclaims the coach.

I look at him blankly and wish I'd gone out for football, where I just could have been maimed for life.

Fuck.

Practice with the Greenwich High School team is much like that of my junior high school team. We do lots of spins, and other stupid exercises, but I don't get as sore the second time around.

I also don't get another erection while wrestling; ice on my balls before practice does the trick.

After a month of practicing six days a week, we're ready for our first meet. I have become a fairly decent wrestler, and am going up against guys in the 107 and 114 weight class at practices, and beating them. I start to think that wrestling may indeed be an okay sport.

And I may have some talent. At something.

Our first meet is against Stamford, and I'm up against a guy named Brandon. As I stand in front of his school in my dorky head gear, pussy shorts, and clown shoes, I look at Brandon.

He looks down at his feet and I can tell he's scared, shitless, like me.

I've never wrestled varsity.

Hell, I've only been in one other match my entire life.

The referee asks us if we are both ready as the crowd starts to cheer.

Suddenly, I feel all this adrenaline surge through my veins and I actually stand up taller. I begin to remember what that Taylor guy had whispered to me in junior high, and I want revenge. I want to nail his ass good. Show him I am a great wrestler, and not going to take shit from anyone. I want blood, Taylor's blood.

Of course, the only problem is that it isn't Taylor I'm wrestling, it's some other kid.

Named Brandon.

"Fuck it." I tell myself. "Taylor, Brandon—what's the difference?"

The referee blows the whistle and I go in for the kill right away.

I grab Brandon's legs, knock him to the ground, and have him on his back before he even knows what's happening.

"How do ya like this?" I find myself saying to the kid as he lies on his back.

As the referee begins the final count I whisper to Brandon, "How does it feel to lose, fucker?"

"Three, two one, pin!" yells the referee, then blows his whistle.

I look at the clock. Fifteen seconds have elapsed since the beginning of the match.

"I beat you fast, pussy," I brag to Brandon, as I stand up.

Then I hear him sob. So I look him in the eyes.

Big mistake.

There he is, lying on the mat curled up in a little ball, crying. Tears are running down his bright-red cheeks.

I feel like total shit.

"I'm sorry," I say, and mean it.

But it doesn't matter, the damage is done.

I had taken this kid down and embarrassed him in front of his whole school. I'm an asshole. I had wanted revenge and tried to use Brandon to get it. I had wanted to show everyone what a tough little man I am, and I suppose I did.

"I'm really sorry," I say to Brandon again, as I try helping him to his feet. He just pushes me away, and keeps bawling.

Suddenly I'm surrounded by my entire team along with Coach Mathers. They pick me up in the air and parade me around, chanting, "Fifteen seconds! Fifteen seconds!"

As I look at my team and coach beneath me, and the crowd of people cheering wildly, I suddenly feel very, very alone. I don't want to be around these people, and as soon as they put me down I run into the locker room and stay there for the rest of the match. I never want to see Brandon's face.

Ever again.

*

I stay on the team throughout the tenth grade, but lose every match I'm put in on purpose.

I just don't care anymore.

At the end of the season I get my varsity letter, which is a big red *G*.

But secretly, I wish for something else.

A big letter *P*.

For *Pussy*.

So I'll never forget who and what I became that awful day.

HOW TO SUCCEED
IN OKLAHOMA

"*Oooooo-klahoma*," I SING, AS I watch Susan and her ninth grade breasts heave with every gasp of air, "*where the wind comes sweeping down the plains, where the waving wheat can sure smell sweet, and the wind comes right behind the rain!*"

"*You know we belong to the land*," Susan and her harem of junior-high school harlots sing, "*and that land we belong to is grand!*"

"*And when we say, Yip-eeyo-kiaa*," bellow my pal Shawn and I, as we watch in amazement while Eve Colvin, who has even bigger breasts than Susan, does a cartwheel. "*We're saying you're doing fine Oklahoma, Oklahoma, O-K-L-A-H-O-M-A, Oklahoma. Okay!*"

With that, the crowd of about three hundred students in the school auditorium for the afternoon assembly applaud wildly. Not for us, I'm sure, but for the chicks.

And him.

Stan.

Curly.

The star of the show.

The kid who sings opposite Susan.

The kid who beat me and ten others for the starring role.

The captain of the football team.

The star of the baseball team.

The kid who kicks ass on the wrestling team.

The kid who plays first trumpet.

Stan.

The kid with *one* arm.

The kid who actually has a life.

The kid I think I've come to despise.

*

"Guess what Dad," I say to my father one Sunday afternoon, while he's busy watching me sweep then hose out our three car garage in Greenwich, Connecticut.

"What?" asks my father, as he sits in the shade of a large rock, on his lawn chair, sipping ice tea.

"Our chorus is putting on a musical," I say, excited, " and guess which one it is?"

"Well," he explains," if it isn't *How to Succeed in Business Without Really Trying*, I'm not interested."

"But it's a good play," I insist.

"If it isn't *How to Succeed in Business Without Really Trying* and you don't have the Robert Morse role," he says, "don't bother telling me about it."

But I do anyway, as I hose out the corners of the filthy garage, watching spider webs, spark plugs, and dead mice float by.

"It's *Oklahoma!*," I explain, "the Rogers and Hammerstein musical."

"Uh-huh," he says, more interested in making sure I hose down the walls and floor of the garage.

"And they haven't picked a lead yet, so maybe I'll get it!" I exclaim.

"You?" asks my father, laughing. "Getting Gordon MacRae's part?"

I feel my heart sink.

"Never," he scowls, as he finishes his glass of ice tea and pours himself another.

I feel two feet tall.

"Maybe you can get the Rod Stieger role, Jud," explains my dad, "because he sure is ugly."

I continue to hose down my father's Rolls Royce parking space, saying nothing.

"You know something, you should play Jud," says my dad.

I start to hose where he parks his ugly green Porsche 911-S.

"Because then you'd be killed and I'd be through with you," he explains, smiling.

"Fuck-wad," I mumble under my breath, at a loss for any other words.

"What'd you say?" yells my father.

"Nothing," I say quietly, staring at the ground.

"You're damn right you said nothing," he yells. "Because you are nothing. I have a nothing for a son—a useless nothing."

"Sorry I'm nothing," I moan, sarcastically, as I grab a mop to scrub oil stains.

"That's okay," replies my father. "I have two other sons. Maybe they'll amount to something, even get Robert Morse's role in *How to Succeed in Business Without Really Trying*."

Then he pours himself another glass of iced tea.

*

"George," says Mr. Cummings, our chorus teacher, "you have a really powerful tenor voice. You could be the lead in the musical."

"Really?" I say to the old, balding guy with the big, black glasses. "I could be a lead?"

"Sure," he answers, assuredly, "your voice is so pure. How do you sing such high notes?"

I look at my teacher, sitting behind his desk after class. We're all alone with him.

"I dunno." I answer. "My stepmother says it has something to do with a guy named Hubert."

"Hubert?" asks Mr. Cummings. "Is that your father?"

"No," I answer, "my father's name is Lester."

"Then who's Hubert?" asks Mr. Cummings .

"I dunno," I reply, "but his last name starts with a T because she always calls him by his first name and last initial."

"Huh?" says Mr. Cummings, scratching his bald spot.

"She just says something about me never reaching him. He must be really tall or something," I explain.

Mr. Cummings laughs and tells me to run off to the auditorium where rehearsals for *Oklahoma!* are beginning.

*

Later that afternoon, I find myself sitting next to my pal, Shawn, who spells his name like a girl. I once asked him why he didn't spell it "S-E-A-N," like James Bond did.

"I don't know," he replied. "I think it's because my parents really wanted a girl."

As Shawn and I sit and talk about how we're both going to try out for Curly, *he* walks in.

The kid with one arm.

Stan.

"Aw, fuck," says Shawn, with his flaming red Irish afro and pasty-white face. "Looks like Stan is going out for Curly as well."

"How do you know?" I ask him.

"He's the captain of everything and gets laid more than a carpet. Of course he's gonna go for Curly," answers Shawn.

"Oh," I say.

"Hi guys," says Stan.

We say nothing.

"How you guys doin'?" he asks, looking in our direction.

"Are you talking to us?" Shawn finally asks.

"No, morons, I'm talking to the wall," he replies.

"Oh," I say again.

"Of course I'm talking to you, you little pansies," yells Stan.

"Well then, we're fine," says Shawn. "How are you?"

"Great," says Stan. "I'm gonna be Curly in *Oklahoma!* What parts are you guys going for? The farmer's wives?"

"We want to be Curly, too!" I blurt out.

Stan just looks at me and laughs.

"What's so funny?" I ask the one-armed kid who is much taller than both Shawn and I, and is wearing a long-sleeved white button-up shirt, with one sleeve pinned back at the elbow.

"What's so funny?" asks Stan. "Well, one of you looks like a circus clown," he explains, "and the other is a little Jew."

"Curly could be a Jew," I yell at the kid who resembles a slot-machine. "After all, he's named after his curly hair. Like mine!"

"Ha," says Stan.

"And he could look like a circus clown!" says Shawn.

"You guys are losers," says Stan, and with that, leaves us to go and talk with Susan, who is trying out for the Shirley Jones role, and Eve, who is going for Little Ado Annie.

They both get the parts.

And Stan, of course, gets the role of Curly.

The next day Mr. Cummings announces who gets what role. When I ask him why I'm cast as just a nameless farmer, and Shawn, as "man number two," Mr. Cummings just smiles and says, "ask Hubert T."

Whatever.

*

Rehearsals for *Oklahoma!* last at least three months.

During that time, every weekday after school, we rehearse like crazy.

Even though Shawn and I have just a few lines, we are required to be at every rehearsal because we sing on almost every song.

Our favorite parts of those afternoons are when it's time to square dance with the chicks in the chorus. I have this thing for a girl named Winnie Wilson, and Shawn likes Stephanie Carr. When it comes time to dance, we try and get as close to these living, breathing females as possible.

Once I even grab Winnie's left breast. I tell her it's an accident, that I'm reaching for her hand. I think she knows I'm lying, but smiles anyway.

Shawn has no such luck with Stephanie. She dances as far away from him as possible. She also jokes about the way Shawn spells his name, calling him "Oklahomo."

During this time, I'm also on the wrestling team with Stan, the one-armed "killing machine," according to our coach.

Stan wrestles the same way every match. When the whistle blows, he throws his nub into the opponents neck and trips him with the opposite foot. Then, when the guy is down on the ground,

Stan gets the guy in a headlock with his half-an-arm and turns him over. Then he pins him. The whole match usually lasts thirty seconds or so.

"That guy is a killing machine," says the coach after every match. "Why can't you guys go tough like him? He's got one arm!"

We're used to hearing that, the one-arm bit.

Every coach and teacher say the same thing. Why can't any of us be like Stan, the one-armed kid?

And, of course, they have a good point.

Stan is amazing.

While playing baseball, if a ball is hit in his direction, he catches it in his mitt, throws the ball up in the air and tucks his mitt beneath his chin, catches the ball, and throws it to where it needs to go.

And he never misses.

He does the same in football, and again, never misses.

He gets so good he becomes the team's quarterback, throwing the pigskin like a guided missile.

He's incredible.

Stan is also amazing on the trumpet, and lets everyone know it.

During rehearsals, he plays incredible solos. Every girl fawns over him and it makes some of us boys ill. I remember bitching about it to my father, who tells me I'm a sick fuck for being jealous of a kid with one arm. He also tells me that if I don't shut up, I may end up with one arm as well.

*

One day, after a long afternoon rehearsal, I find myself alone in the boys' room with Stan.

"How's it going, Jew?" Stan asks, as he washes his hand.

"Do you even know my real name?" I ask him, annoyed.

"Why should I?" he replies.

"Because, besides being in chorus with you, I'm also in classes and on the wrestling team with you," I explain.

"So?" says Stan, "big fucking deal."

"Well, my name is George," I say, defiant, "not Jew."

Then I stick my hand out to shake his.

Then I realize what I'm doing, but it's too late.

My right arm is already extended, and Stan doesn't have one.

"What are you trying to do, Jew?" yells Stan, and with that, jabs his nub into my neck.

Hard.

"Sorry," I wheeze, but it's too late. I see the fury in Stan's eyes.

"I'm gonna kick your faggot ass," he screams.

Then, of course, he does. After alternating between his nub and his fist against my face a few times, he trips me with his left leg and gets on top of me.

"Please stop," I cry, as tears and snot roll down the sides of my face.

"Fuck you," is his reply, as he nub-slaps me on each side of my face, over and over.

"I'm really sorry," I cry. "I didn't mean to imply you were missing anything!!"

"The only thing you'll be missing," yells Stan, as he stands up and starts kicking me, "are your teeth!"

Stan continues to kick my ass, and finally leaves me, a bloody pulp on the bathroom floor. After I finish crying, I'm too ashamed to take the bus home, so I walk.

*

Finally, the week comes when we are to perform four shows. Three of them are daytime shows, during school hours. Two are at other schools, and one is at ours. Then there's the night show.

That's the one that scares me.

Because my stepmother, along with my brothers and sisters, will be there, as well as my dad.

And I didn't want them to see me on stage.

In a bit part, wearing brown corduroy pants instead of blue jeans because my dad's too cheap to buy me a pair.

But the big night slowly arrives anyway, and everyone is nervous.

Our parents are there to see us.

I even see Stan twitching around before the show.

The band starts playing and when the overture ends the curtains go up and our final, and most important, show begins.

"*There's a bright golden haze on the meadow,*" sings Stan in a beautiful voice, exposing the audience to his cowboy hat, leather chaps, and one arm.

All at once.

"*There's a bright golden haze on the meadow,*" Stan continues.

Some parents and kids gasp.

"*The corn is as high as an elephants eye, and it looks like it's climbing clear up to the sky,*" sings Stan, ignoring the crowd.

We all join in on "Oh What a Beautiful Morning," and the crowd, now over their shock, goes nuts.

They clap, whistle, and cheer us on.

We continue the musical and by the end, everyone is singing along.

"*Oooook-lahoma,*" we hear the audience sing along with us, as we smile.

And it feels so good.

*

After the show, and a standing ovation, lots of our parents come backstage.

I watch as Shawn hugs his mom and dad, both of whom have curly red afros.

I smile as Winnie introduces me to her mother and brother.

I also look and listen as Stan's Dad comes backstage to congratulate his son.

"You did okay," the father tells his one-armed son, "but next time I think you could do a lot better."

Stan says nothing.

"You have to prove that having one arm doesn't make you a loser," his father continues.

As Stan's father lectures him, I can see a single tear well up in the kid's eye.

I feel terrible.

Then Stan catches me staring at him. The look on his face is something I never want to see again.

Ever.

*

That night, on the way out to our brown-paneled station wagon, my father pulls me aside in the parking lot and talks to me.

Alone.

"George," he says, "that kid who plays Curly, he's got only one arm."

"Uh-huh," I say, thinking about how Stan's dad must find disappointment in everything his son does.

"Well," continues my father, "what I'm trying to say is I'm glad your chorus didn't do *How to Succeed in Business Without Really Trying*."

When I ask him why, he says "A one-armed Robert Morse would have been simply awful."

"Fuck-wad," I mumble under my breath, once again.

"What'd you say?" yells my dad.

"Fuck-wad," I say loudly and clearly.

"That's what I thought," he says, and with that, hits me in the mouth so hard my gums start bleeding.

*

The next day at school I see Stan in the cafeteria, seated at a table full of cheerleaders, and I smile.

He sees me smiling at him, and just in the very corners of his mouth, smiles back.

"What are you smiling about?" asks Shawn, seeing me look at Stan.

"In a land of men with two arms, the one-armed man can still be king," I reply.

"What are you talking about?" asks Shawn.

"Nothing," I tell him. With that I motion for him to follow me to a table where Winnie and Stephanie are sitting, waiting for us to join them.

THE GIFT

So, THERE I AM, ON the roof of my house, trying to do my best Lee Harvey Oswald impression. It 's really hot and the sun's glare doesn't help my aim as I look through the sights of my Crossman 760 Rifle. In view, about 350 feet away, is my mortal enemy; a guy who causes me a lot of grief; a guy who accuses me of lying; a guy who, in the past, has inflicted upon me enough physical and mental pain to make me reach my breaking point.

But now, as I steady the barrel of the gun, I'm going to get even. It's payback time. Just one little squeeze of the trigger, and he'll know that fucking with George Tabb is a huge mistake, a mistake he'll never forget. I figure I'll go down in history as a big hero or something. So what if I'm only fourteen and the guy at the end of my sights is my father.

*

But things weren't always that way. Not at all.

Like most fathers and sons, our differences grew with age. We—or I—tried to settle these differences, but eventually they became way too big. As a young boy, I wanted so much to be like my father; he was a strong man, a provider, and in my naive eyes, a good person. But the more I got to know him—or the smarter I became—the less I wanted to be him. It took me a while to come to that conclusion. And during that while, I learned a lot about myself, who I wanted to be, and who I definitely didn't want to be.

My first memories of my father are rather pleasant. I remember waking up early on weekend mornings when I was around two, and my father putting me in the basket of his bicycle and peddling me out to Coney Island. I remember clearly the white basket with the big, colored plastic flowers, and the smell of my dad's cologne mixed with the early morning air. When we arrived at Coney Island, he'd take me on all sorts of rides and buy me a hot dog or hamburger along the boardwalk. We'd sit there, father and son, with the sun warming our backs, and somehow I felt as if I was one with the world, even though I was only two.

That feeling didn't last very long.

*

My first big falling out with my father came around the the age of four.

My brother, Luke, and I were out on our gravel driveway in Long Island doing the usual kid stuff, throwing rocks at each other and at our youngest brother, Sam.

Suddenly, we got the idea that these rocks, or bits of gravel, would be put to better use filling up that little hole on the side of the family's station wagon. We unscrewed the cap and smelled the wonderful odor of gasoline. Luke found rocks small enough to fit in the hole, and we started to drop them in, one by one.

"Plink, plink, plink, kerplunk!" we heard, and then jumped up and down with glee. I guess we imagined that these rocks were making journeys into other universes, and I wished that somehow we could follow.

The next day my father came home from work in the middle of the day, red-faced and shaking. I overheard him explain to my mother that the car quit halfway to work, and when he took it into the station to have it looked at, they found half our driveway in the gas tank. My mom kind of laughs, then covers her mouth with the back of her wrist so my father can't see. Eventually she calms him down, and all is well. But that's the last time she's able to save us from our father. Shortly thereafter, my parents got a divorce.

*

Like most fathers, mine held down a steady job, and a good one at that. My dad was a stockbroker. And he was good, very good. Well, not him actually—more like his partner, Richie. See, my dad and Richie were trading stocks during the late sixties and early seventies—the golden years. The term "insider trading" didn't really carry much weight, so Richie and my dad made a bundle in the business. I remember watching Richie dance up and down on his desk, with rolls of ticker-tape running through his hands, yelling that he just made another million. My dad would smile, then go back to balancing ledger sheets with his Blackwing #2 pencils

*

When I was old enough to understand that my father worked hard and was a success, I wanted to be like him. Even though I wasn't happy with his choice of a new wife and the fact that I couldn't go live with my real mom.

I felt he was a good man, overall, the sort of guy who worked hard, and typified the American dream. He was like the characters I got to know from comic books and television shows. You see, I spent most of my free time with my nose stuck in a comic book, or my eyes fixed on the television, living in a sort of fantasy world.

And I loved Spiderman.

Batman, too.

I even loved that sissy in the red cape, Superman.

They were all heroes to me.

Role models.

They had immeasurable strength, and constantly saved people from terrible fates. They somehow managed to lead dual lives, hiding their superhuman identity, and acting normal to the out-side world; they were important.

So were the characters on television shows like *Happy Days*, *The Brady Bunch*, and *Gilligan's Island*. In each of these shows, the characters tried to be moral, and to do the right thing at any cost. Mr. Brady always told his kids when they did wrong and teach them what was right. From Jan getting her glasses, to Greg's happy exile to the attic, Mr. Brady was the man. He knew what to say and do in order to make his kids feel good and grow up well-adjusted and happy with the world.

The same went for Mr. C. on *Happy Days*. Richie came to him for advice, or to the Fonz, who was, in a way, a surrogate father to all the kids, and to me.

When it came to *Gilligan's Island*, we all knew they'd never get off that damned place, but it didn't matter. They were all one big family. They learned about each other, the world, and how to act in it. It was a sort of microcosm of the earth, there on *Gilligan's Island*.

*

Then there was my house and the life I led there. As I got

older, my dad spent more and more time at work. And when he did come home, it wasn't pleasant. My stepmother, Cybil, had a way of winding him up then setting him loose on my brothers and me. If we didn't do something like take out the trash, correctly clean the dishes, or even if we *looked* at her funny—she'd push my dad's buttons until he popped a fuse. Then he'd beat the hell out of my brothers or me.

And it was usually me.

I began, emotionally, to rely more on the superheroes. I took my dad's abuse, yet somehow managed to lead a normal life. Or, at least to appear as I did, just like Peter Parker or Bruce Wayne. Yet, somehow, I still believed my father was a good man; a bit misguided, but good.

He did take us to ball games once in a while, with his father— my grandfather. He did take us on family trips, and he once even tried to have that father-and-son "sex speech."

"George," explained my father, "in sex, anything goes."

I just nodded my head, not knowing what the fuck he was talking about.

"Do you understand me?" he asked.

Again, I nodded my head, clueless.

I was eleven years old, but I wish I'd known.

I wish I'd known that my father liked to wear women's underwear.

That he liked to wear them under his business suits.

Had I known, I probably would have been in awe of him. Superman, Batman, and even Spiderman wore funny underwear under their clothes, and they ruled.

*

As I got a bit older, I began to understand what my dad was doing work-wise, well, wasn't exactly right. I'd hear from other kids that my dad was a "dirty Jew" and a thief. They'd say my dad was crooked and robbed people, and that was why he was rich. I'd look at them and wonder what their fathers did to make them rich enough to live in Greenwich, Connecticut, too.

When I asked my father about what the kids said, he told me they didn't know what they were talking about. That they were talking "bubbermices." My dad liked that old word. It means nonsense, nothing, crazy talk, untruthfulness. I thought my dad made it up, but later learned he didn't.

Anyway, his defensive tone told me that he was the one who was actually "talking bubbermices."

Eventually my father got out of the insider-trading business and started making bicycle parts. He and a partner opened a factory about ten miles away in Stamford, and hired my brothers and me to work there. Using toxic chemicals like Loctite and working side by side with active members of the Black Panther Party.

One day this Rasta guy, Mike, tells me that my white-man father is exploiting the poor black man and that the Black Panthers are going to get even. He explained that they were going to attack the factory and get the pay they deserved. He also told us we were sons of a slave driver, that our father was a white satan.

That night, I told my father that the Black Panthers were going to attack the factory, and that Mike had called him a white satan. Then I asked him why giant cats would want to attack a bicycle parts company, and wondered aloud how he could be Satan. He told me not to make up stuff and then hit me in the jaw.

Hard.

I didn't say another word.

The next night they tied up my father's partner and robbed the place.

When my father heard about it he asked me why I didn't tell him what Mike had said. I told him I did, but he wouldn't listen. He told me it was my fault for not making him listen, and it was then I knew my dad was kind of crazy.

It wasn't like I hadn't seen it before, what with all the beatings and outrageous lies he told me about my mother and stepfather, but finally it began to sink in that he really didn't have a great grip on reality. He was a bitter man, and not very moral one.

It was then I completely buried myself in television. Since I lived in a large house with no neighbors nearby, I had no one to really turn to. But there was always Tom Bosley, Mr. C. on *Happy Days*, and the *Gilligan's Island* bunch. I'd sit in front of the tube, feeling safe and secure. Everything they did was moral and right, and I'd learn from them. Every time I tried to learn something from my dad, it either didn't make any sense, or was two-faced. And that, I couldn't stand.

Then one Saturday morning, when I was about thirteen or fourteen, my life changed.

Forever.

*

I wake up early that day, as I usually do on weekends, to get a head start on my chores. Every weekend it was my job, and my brothers', to muck the horse shit and piss out of ten stalls, then mow fourteen acres of land with a hand mower, one with no engine, like in the old days, the kind my father told me he used to use, the kind that gave him muscles.

Even though he grew up in Brooklyn.

In Flatbush.

Without a lawn.

But this Saturday was different. When I go downstairs to pour myself a bowl of Fruit Loops, and check out the Christian puppet television show *Davey and Goliath*, before getting a start on my chores, I find my dad in the kitchen, smiling. It's strange, he doesn't smile often.

My dad continues smiling, just staring at me.

Like he's finally gone insane.

Sos finally I say, "Good morning, dad."

He remains silent, smiling.

Finally my dad speaks, after following me into the television room where I start to watch the episode where Davey sneaks into a cave and falls down a hole, and Goliath, his dog, saves him.

"I got you a present," says my dad, with the stupid grin still on his face.

I get excited.

My dad got me a present.

Maybe it's a radio-controlled plane or car.

Maybe it's a camera.

Maybe it's even just a new pair of sneakers.

Something.

Something that says "I love you."

Anything.

"Hurry up and eat your cereal," barks my dad, "I want to give you your present."

I eat the rest of my Fruit Loops as fast as I can, and then my dad tells me to follow him. I do.

He leads me outside, down the driveway, and to our barn. There he leads me to one of our three garage doors.

"Behind this door is your present," he says, smiling and proud.

I feel my heart begin to race.

My dad got me a car.

I'm still too young for it, but soon I'll be able to drive. Then I can be free of him, my stepmother, and my horrid existence.

"Are you ready for your present?" asks my dad as he bends down to open the garage door.

"Yes, dad," I say, and for some reason remember the smell of my dad's cologne and the warmth of the sun on our backs at Coney Island, all those years ago.

"Okay, well, here it is!" exclaims my dad, and, with that, he pulls open the garage door.

I must have looked like a zombie from *Night of the Living Dead* right then. I feel my jaw drop to my knees and my brain go into some sort of suspended animation. I think I start to drool.

"What do you think?" asks my dad, excited.

I say nothing.

I just look.

In the garage.

At it.

"Well?" asks my dad, very happy with himself.

What could I say.

In front of me is a brand-new, chrome handled, three-speeds-on-top, push-power lawn mower, from Sears.

"Umm," I stammer.

"It's got three speed settings for the blades, and can cut grass very quickly," explains my father. "It should help you out a lot and cut your mowing time at least by a quarter, if not in half."

"Uhhh," I stutter.

"And," he adds, "it's all yours and your brothers'. Take care of it!"

"Ummm," I say.

"I know," says my dad, smile beaming, "you want to say thank you. You are lucky to have a father like me!"

"Umm, yeah," I manage to say before I feel the Fruit Loops make their way up my throat, then back down again.

"Well, you're welcome," says my dad, and with that he walks away proudly.

About a half-hour later I have the thing up and running, and start to cut one of our many lawns. The thing is really loud and hard to push, almost as hard as the handmower. The only difference is that this one has blades that spin on their own. But it's heavier.

About a half-hour later, I'm mowing around our swimming pool when suddenly I feel the mower buck like a horse and make a really funny noise.

Then the lawn mower stops, dead.

I try to restart it by yanking on the cord, but nothing happens. I try again, and again.

Still, nothing.

Eventually, I turn the thing over to see what has happened. I must have run over a rock, a big one. One that was embedded in the ground and thus impossible to see under the tall grass. The blades must have hit the rock, because they are twisted up like limp spaghetti.

I feel bad for destroying my dad's new lawn mower, but at the same time I kind of feel happy; he deserves it.

I run to the house and into my dad's study, and tell him to come look at the lawn mower. He follows me out to the broken machine, saying nothing. I show him the new blue-and-black Sears power mower, with the three-speeds-on-top, and the twisted blades below. He takes one look at it and punches me in the face so hard I think I'm unconscious for about a minute.

When I come to, I see my dad leaning over the machine cursing me out. He sees me looking at him and swears at me to my face. I think I start crying. Then I feel blood from above my eye run past my nose and mix with my snot, before going into my mouth.

"You little piece of shit," my dad says to me, "you did this on purpose. You broke my gift."

I try telling him I didn't, but can't get words out, only moans.

"I give you a fucking present, and this is how you repay me?" my father yells. "Stand up, George."

I do what I'm told.

Then my dad hits me again in the face, really hard. Once again, I collapse to the ground.

"Go to your fucking room and stay there for the rest of the weekend," screams my dad. "I can't trust you anymore."

I do what I'm told, crying all the way, feeling horrible, like I let my dad down.

But I also feel anger. Mr. C. would never do this. Spiderman's Aunt May would never treat Peter Parker like this. And there was no way in hell Mike Brady was going to pull this crap. As I enter my house, my stepmother sees me crying and bleeding and just laughs.

I sit in my room for about an hour, looking at a Spiderman comic book, sobbing all over it. Then I get an idea.

The next thing I know I'm removing the screen window in the upstairs bathroom and making my way out onto our roof with my Crossman 760. I'm fuming, and am going to make my father pay for what he just did to me.

Fucker.

*

So, there I am, on the roof of my house, trying to do my best Lee Harvey Oswald impression. It's really hot, and the sun's glare doesn't help my aim as I look through the sights of my rifle.

I look at him as he bends over that Sears mower, trying to fix it with some wrenches and other tools. I feel myself smile as the cross-hairs of the sight line up with his head. I have pumped the gun about twenty times, and loaded in a lead pellet instead of a BB. The gun is ready to fire at full-force and, hopefully, it will put a hole in my father's head the size of a golf ball, at least.

As I take aim, I feel a sense of power rage through my veins. Finally, I'm taking control of my life and control of him. I've grown to not like him, or trust him at all. This man is my father, yet he is someone I don't respect and don't want to be anything like, at all. He is dishonest, uncaring, and unlike the fantasy people I strive to be. At that second I realize I would never be, and could never be, like my father.

I realize I'm my own person, raised according to different values, values he could never understand.

And then I pull the trigger.

The pellet stings him really hard in the neck and he runs around the backyard yelling that a bee or wasp has stung him.

And I think he believed that until the day he died.

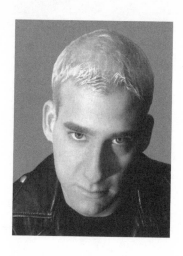

Born in Brooklyn, mostly raised in Greenwich, Connecticut, George Tabb was sentenced to play right field for a series of kiddie baseball teams. His parents got a divorce when he was five. At almost seventeen, Tabb drove a car for a second time, from New York to Tallahassee, towing two horses with his brother. There he attended the University of Florida and started one of Florida's first hardcore bands, Roach Motel, who went on to tour with Black Flag and the Dead Kennedys. After departing college rather hastily, Tabb moved to New York where he continued to build his name as a punk rock icon, with bands like False Prophets, Letch Patrol, The Gynecologists, Iron Prostate, and Furious George. He also served in the Ramones for a short time. Tabb still plays, writes, and tours, not necessarily in that order.

Thanks to: Wendy, Nick, Richard, Sarah, Ammi & the rest of the Soft Skull Crew, Fly, the Smith Family, Andy Krents, Esq., and John Strausbaugh for the kindest of words.